Third Edition

Instructor's Manual for

CORTEZ PETERS'

AN INDIVIDUALIZED DIAGNOSTIC/ PRESCRIPTIVE METHOD FOR DEVELOPING ACCURACY AND SPEED

Cortez Peters
Undefeated Champion Typist

GLENCOE
McGraw-Hill
New York, New York
Columbus, Ohio
Woodland Hills, California
Peoria, Illinois

Instructor's Manual for
Cortez Peters' Championship Keyboarding Drills, Third Edition

Imprint 1999

Send all inquiries to:

Glencoe/McGraw-Hill
936 Eastwind Drive
Westerville, OH 43081

(800) 848-1567

Printed in the United States of America.

ISBN 0-02-801201-1

5 6 7 8 9 10 045 04 03 02 01 00 99

Contents

Background of a Champion

. . . Why You Should Use This Program!

The author, Cortez Peters, Jr., was born into a world championship typewriting family and, like his father, was an undefeated typewriting champion. He believed he was probably more knowledgeable than any keyboarding author about the best way to develop speed with a high degree of accuracy because of his championship typing background.

Although it is possible to increase a keyboarder's accuracy in four weeks or less, it is difficult and time-consuming to build high speed. By *high speed,* the author means a speed of 80–120 net words a minute. It is not difficult to get a student to progress from 20–40 net words a minute, but it becomes increasingly more difficult as the student's speed increases. At the world championship level of proficiency, the fastest keyboarder in the world can practice 4–8 hours a day for six months only to see an increase of 1 net word a minute. This is the ultimate of skill development. Even though developing an employable skill does not require that degree of discipline, the author, nevertheless, presents the activities and procedures that produce superior keyboarders and sequences these activities to enable the student to attain high speed with a high degree of accuracy.

There are four effective methods for developing speed; namely, championship techniques, concentration, rhythmic keying, and conscientious practicing. These four methods should all be used together. One without the other will not be effective.

The first and most important method is acquiring **championship techniques.** The author's father learned world championship typing techniques from George Hossfield, a world champion typist during the era of Cortez Peters, Sr. Cortez Peters, Sr., learned from Hossfield that every motion in typing should be executed in a certain way, and that the "certain way" had evolved into a *technique.* If Cortez Peters, Sr., had not learned these world championship techniques, he probably would have remained an 80-net-word-a-minute typist instead of becoming the fastest typist of all time on a manual typewriter. Cortez Peters, Sr., practiced 3 hours every day using the newly acquired techniques—techniques that enabled him to reach the status of World Champion Typist.

Cortez Peters, Jr., author of this program, saw world championship keyboarding techniques most of his life and felt that these techniques varied considerably from those illustrated in practically every other keyboarding book. Therefore, in Peters' opinion, acquiring these world championship keyboarding techniques was the most important aspect of speed development. The author developed a Technique Evaluation Chart (see page 41 in this manual) for your convenience in evaluating your students' techniques. This weekly evaluation during corrective practice days will make your students *technique conscious* and, as a result, will enhance their keyboarding speed development.

The second most important technique is **concentration.** To perfect concentration, students should key on a letter-by-letter basis, saying each letter to themselves as they strike it. This will enable them to key for duplication rather than comprehension.

The third most important method of speed development is **rhythmic keying.** When Cortez Peters, Jr., learned to type, he had the advantage of having a world champion typist pace his keystroking rhythm. When Cortez Peters, Jr., was typing 30 words a minute (WAM), his father would sit by his side and key the same copy at the rate of 40 WAM. Cortez Peters, Jr., would listen to his father's rhythm for several minutes and would then begin to key right along with him, matching his father stroke for stroke. Cortez Peters, Sr., would leave the room while his son continued keying at that rate. Cortez Peters, Sr., would return 15 minutes later to see how well his son had mastered the pace. This was how Cortez Peters, Sr., led his son from the rate of 30 WAM to 140 WAM, a rate that Cortez Peters, Jr., could key on a manual typewriter when he was only 16 years old.

To duplicate this "pacing" technique, Cortez Peters, Jr., developed a set of Rhythm Development Drills that you can use to accomplish with your students what his father accomplished with him. If your students are using the CD-ROM component, these pacing drills are available from the menu. If not, the pacing drills are available on tape in the Rhythm-Development Drills package. The Rhythm-Development Drills Chart (page 42 in this manual) should be used to evaluate the student's performance and provide motivation for continued practice. Instructions for using the drills can be found on page 30 under the heading "Rhythm-Development Drills."

The fourth most important technique is **conscientious practicing.** The student should be encouraged to practice with enthusiasm and with the knowledge that practicing the drills in the correct sequence and in the correct way will produce the desired results!

Components of the Program

This program has five components: the text, two software components (disk format or CD-ROM), Rhythm-Development Tapes, and an instructor's manual. The CD-ROM component also contains the Rhythm-Development Drills. The synergism of this diagnostic/prescriptive process, the championship techniques, and the motivational techniques produce sensational results.

Program Overview

. . . A Champion's Skillbuilding Philosophy

The *Cortez Peters' Championship Keyboarding Drills* program is a comprehensive and definitive diagnostic approach to building keyboarding skill. The program is designed to build speed while maintaining a high degree of accuracy and accomplishes this through its diagnostic approach of identifying individual keystroking weaknesses and prescribing specific drills to correct those weaknesses. This skillbuilding program can be implemented anytime after the keyboard has been taught, is ideal for use in a five- or six-week block of time, and can be used in conjunction with any keyboarding program.

Cortez Peters' Championship Keyboarding Drills program builds skill through planned repetition of activities. This repetition is called a **skillbuilding cycle.** The program was originally developed to fit the schedule of a class meeting one period a day (40–45 minutes), five days a week, five to six weeks during one semester or one quarter. It takes five, 40–60 minute classes (3–5 hours) to complete one cycle. This is important for you to know because not all courses follow the standard one-period-a-day, five-days-a-week schedule, and knowing how much time to allow for each activity will enable you to create your own schedule while continuing to achieve the results the author intended.

The four activities that make up a cycle and around which the time is divided are the Pretest, the charting activities, the corrective practice, and the Posttest. The Pretest determines a starting point in both speed and accuracy skill. Charting the results of the Pretest is the cornerstone of this program because from it flows the corrective practice—the activity that will take up most of the time in the cycle.

Charting the results of the Pretest (1) identifies a student's keyboarding weaknesses in accuracy and speed, and (2) prescribes the practice drills designed to correct those weaknesses. Charting also serves as a means for comparing Pretest and Posttest results. This comparison will indicate the effectiveness of the corrective practice and will provide the student with the incentive to continue conscientious practicing. The complete cycle of Pretest, charting, corrective practice, and Posttest should be repeated five to six consecutive times.

Another activity that can be added to the cycle is the pacing drills (Rhythm-Development). These pacing drills are available on tape or in the CD-ROM component. Instructions on using these drills can be found on page 35 under the heading "Rhythm-Development Drills."

Program Overview

. . . The Cycle Activities Explained

Warmup

It is suggested that each day begin with 5 minutes of warmup. This is especially true of Pretest and Posttest days when a 5-Minute Timed Writing and a Diagnostic Test are given.

Pretest

Students will take a Pretest that consists of two attempts on the same 5-Minute Timed Writing (with the option of taking only one attempt if the student achieves any of three Honor Roll papers) and a 1-minute timing on each of ten different Diagnostic Test sentences.

Note: Starting with the second Pretest 5-Minute Timed Writing, if the student does poorly on accuracy—that is, makes ten or more errors on any 5-Minute Pretest Timed Writing *and* exceeds maximum errors allowed in five or more categories—you may wish to instruct him or her to skip the Diagnostic Test and do the corrective practice prescribed on Chart 2, which is found on page 13 in the text. Under these conditions, the student should not be working on speed until accuracy problems are better controlled.

The student will then chart the results (charting is done automatically if the student is using the software or CD-ROM components) of the better 5-Minute Timed Writing as well as the results of each of the ten Diagnostic Test Sentences. Each student will record the results of the better 5-Minute Timed Writing on Chart 1 (the Speed and Accuracy Graph) that serves as a visual record of a student's progress in both speed and accuracy on the 5-Minute Timed Writings. As the student sees progress (an increase in speed and a reduction in errors), he or she will be motivated to continue practicing enthusiastically and conscientiously. The student will recognize that it is this practice that increases speed and reduces errors; thus, the student recognizes that the program is working and excellent keyboarding skill is being developed. The "better" of two timed writings is explained on page 6 of the text under the heading "Agenda of Cycle Activities."

The student will then fill in Chart 2 (Misstroke Analysis Chart, found on page 13 of the text). This chart determines deficiencies in *accuracy:* it categorizes errors, identifies individual keystroking weaknesses and error patterns, and prescribes the Accuracy Studies that should be keyed as corrective practice. Once the student identifies which Accuracy Studies need to be keyed, he or she must prioritize the sequence in which they are keyed. The proper sequence is identified on the chart itself, but primarily it is as follows: concentration errors first; letters-of-the-alphabet next (doing first the letter having the most errors, then the letter with the second highest number of errors, then the letter with the third highest number of errors, etc.); punctuation, shifting, and spacing errors (doing first the one having the highest number of errors, then the one having the second highest number of errors, then the one having the least number of errors); finger errors (again, highest number of errors to least number of errors); hand errors (highest number of errors to least number of errors); and total errors last.

Finally, the student will complete Chart 3 (Speed and Accuracy Analysis, found on page 16 of the text) with the results from the Diagnostic Test sentences. This chart identifies deficiencies in both accuracy and speed. Once all information has been recorded, and the student identifies which Accuracy Studies and Speed Studies will need to be keyed as corrective practice, he or she must prioritize the sequence in which they are keyed. The student should prioritize the Accuracy Studies assignments first, then the Speed Studies assignments. The proper sequence is as follows: the sentence with the highest number of errors should be keyed first, then the sentence with the second highest number of errors, then the sentence with the third highest number of errors, etc. Accuracy Studies from both Charts 2 and 3 should be keyed before the Speed Studies (prescribed only from Chart 3). If the student has excellent accuracy on any 5-Minute Timed Writing, as indicated by an Accuracy Honor Roll paper, a Speed Honor Roll paper, or a Super Honor Roll paper, instruct him or her to skip the corrective practice prescribed on Chart 2 (Misstroke Analysis) as well as the corrective practice for accuracy prescribed on Chart 3 (Speed and Accuracy Analysis) and go directly to the Speed Studies prescribed on Chart 3. (Note that all Honor Roll papers require 0–1 errors and matching, exceeding by 5 WAM, or coming within 3 WAM of the most current 5-Minute Timed Writing.)

The directions for completing each chart accompanies that chart. The Pretest and charting activities should take approximately 40–60 minutes to complete.

Note: Once the student has eliminated all speed deficiencies or has only 1 speed deficiency on a Pretest Diagnostic Test, he should select the minimum speed goal for each sentence from the next speed level (Minimum 1-Minute Speeds for Diagnostic Tests table) when taking the next Diagnostic Test.

Corrective Practice

It does not matter which days of the week the Pretest and Posttest are given as long as adequate corrective practice hours intervene. In most cases, it will be necessary to have 3 consecutive corrective practice hours during each cycle. If your class meets only 4 hours a week, instead of 5, then you may have to allow only 2 hours for corrective practice in order to complete a cycle within one week. On the other hand, it is not necessary to complete a cycle within one week, so you may wish to continue the corrective practice into the first day of the next week and administer the Posttest the last half of that day; or you may wish to use the second, as well as the first, day of that second week to finish up the cycle. These options are indicated on the Sample Schedules (see pages 12–17).

Just remember to allow adequate time between Pretest and Posttest days for the students to key the drills that will correct their keystroking weaknesses—3 hours are preferred, 2 hours are the minimum, and 5 hours are the maximum.

Corrective practice drills are taken from the Accuracy Studies prescribed from Charts 2 and 3, and Speed Studies are prescribed from Chart 3. Since accuracy is more important than speed, students should key the Accuracy Studies in sequence as prescribed by Chart 2 first and then the Accuracy Studies in sequence as prescribed by Chart 3. Students should key all of the Accuracy Studies from both charts before proceeding to the Speed Studies prescribed by Chart 3. If students have enough time to key the Speed Studies, they should do so in the sequence prescribed by Chart 3.

In addition to the Accuracy Studies and Speed Studies, you should reserve the last 10–15 minutes of each corrective practice hour for students to take 1-minute timings on the Skill-Development Paragraphs (see page 58 in the text). The paragraphs should be keyed in sequence, beginning with the 20 WAM paragraph. Each time a student keys a paragraph in 1 minute without making an error, he or she should record the achievement on Chart 4 (Record of Skill-Development Paragraphs, found on page 19 in the text). Directions accompany Chart 4. After recording results on Chart 4, the student should proceed to the paragraph with the next higher speed. Chart 4 does not prescribe corrective practice; it only records the successful completion of the Skill-Development Paragraphs at the various speed levels. If a speed plateau is reached on these 1-minute paragraphs, inform the student that in order to progress, he or she should key each line of the paragraph (on a line-by-line basis) 10 times and each word on which an error was made 25 times. Activities to break speed plateaus should also be done during corrective practice hours.

The student will be allowed only five or ten attempts on the paragraphs each corrective practice day. You, the teacher, will decide how many attempts are allowed in one day under the **Options Menu** at the Log-on Screen. The student may use all of his or her attempts on only one paragraph or on several paragraphs, depending on how successful he or she is with each paragraph. Nevertheless, the student should not move on to the next paragraph until successfully completing the current one.

Posttest

Students will take a Posttest that consists of two attempts on the same 5-Minute Timed Writing that was taken in the Pretest and the same Pretest Diagnostic Test. (If a student has earned an Honor Roll paper, he or she has the option of taking only one 5-minute Timed Writing.) The students will (1) record the results of the better 5-Minute Timed Writing on Chart 1 and *in the upper part only of Chart 2* and (2) record the results of each of the ten Diagnostic Test Sentences on Chart 3. No corrective practice is assigned from the Posttest, which serves only as a means of comparison to the Pretest to see what progress has been made in both accuracy and speed. It indicates the effectiveness of the corrective practice. Seeing improved results will motivate the student to continue conscientious practicing.

Once the Posttest has been given, it is your responsibility to carefully analyze the progress of each class in order to determine whether it will be necessary to allow an extra day (no more than two extra days) of corrective practicing in each cycle. Therefore, you are required to make a subjective judgment on the progress of the class and, if necessary, to make minor adjustments in the management of the program.

This process of testing, charting results, diagnosing errors, prescribing specific practice drills, and retesting produces a completely individualized skillbuilding program. The amount of work each student will have to do will depend on how skillful he or she is at keying. The more skill the student has, the fewer errors he or she will make; and the fewer the errors, the less time he or she will have to spend on corrective practice. Be sure to emphasize this to the students so they will understand the importance (and immense benefits) of keying for accuracy.

Scheduling of Cycle Activities

. . . To Fit Your Course Schedule

Course schedules vary from the number of weeks allotted for the course to the number of days per week and the number of hours per day that the class meets. Since no one agenda will serve all schedules, you should determine how the cycle will fit into your own schedule. To help you structure your schedule, a blank Schedule for Class Activities form is provided on pages 44–45. Make as many copies of the blank schedule as you need, and schedule each activity by recording a starting time for that activity for the appropriate day. Remember, the skillbuilding cycle consists of certain activities performed in a specific sequence for a recommended length of time. The cycle activities and their sequence remain constant; the length of time allotted to each activity and the amount of time between activities may vary depending on your course schedule. A cycle will require approximately 3–5 hours, depending on the amount of time you have allotted to each activity, to complete. Whether you complete a cycle in one week or spread the cycle over several weeks depends on your course schedule.

Although your schedule will be unique for your class situation, you should follow the "Scheduling Guidelines" on page 11 in order to maintain the integrity and intent of Cortez Peters' skillbuilding philosophy.

Refer to the "Agenda of Cycle Activities" on pages 5–7 of the text or "Program Overview . . . The Cycle Activities Explained" on pages 6–9 of this manual to reinforce your understanding of the skillbuilding cycle.

Scheduling Guidelines

1. Follow the recommended time allowances for each activity as suggested below.

ACTIVITY	RECOMMENDED TIME ALLOWANCE
Pretest and Charting	45–60 minutes
Corrective Practice	2 hours minimum; 3 hours recommended; 5 hours maximum
Skill-Development Paragraphs and Charting	Last 10–15 minutes of each corrective practice hour
Posttest and Charting	45–60 minutes

2. Make sure the skillbuilding cycles are complete.
3. Allow 3–5 consecutive hours for a cycle.
4. Begin each day with a 5-minute warmup.
5. Allow a minimum of 2 consecutive hours of corrective practice time between the Pretest and Posttest; 3 hours are preferred; 5 hours are the maximum.
6. Reserve the last 10–15 minutes of each corrective practice hour for work on the Skill-Development Paragraphs.
7. If Rhythm-Development Drills are used to increase speed and accuracy through rhythmic keystroking, introduce them as soon as the student has completed three full skillbuilding cycles and has achieved a 35 GWAM speed on a 5-Minute Timed Writing. The same drill should be used for 4–5 consecutive hours and should be *followed* by at least one complete skillbuilding cycle, five cycles if the same drill will be used again. See the heading "Rhythm-Development Drills", on page 30, for details on administering these drills.

Sample Schedule for Class Meeting Two Days a Week / 2 Hours Each Day

SCHEDULE FOR CLASS ACTIVITIES

WEEK	DAY	WARMUP	PRETEST				CORRECTIVE PRACTICE		POSTTEST				Rhythm-Development Drills
			TW Attempt 1	TW Attempt 2	Diagnostic Test	Chart	Accuracy and Speed Studies	Skill-Development Paragraphs	TW Attempt 1	TW Attempt 2	Diagnostic Test	Chart	
	Mon.												
1	Tue.	8:00	8:05	8:10	8:15	9:00	9:15	9:50					
	Wed.												
	Thur.	8:00				8:05	8:05	9:50					
	Fri.												
	Mon.												
2	Tue.	8:00					8:05	8:50	9:05	9:20	9:30	9:45	
	Wed.												
	Thur.	8:00	8:05	8:10	8:15	9:00	9:15	9:50					
	Fri.												
	Mon.												
3	Tue.	8:00					8:05	9:50					
	Wed.												
	Thur.	8:00					8:05	8:50	9:05	9:20	9:30	9:45	
	Fri.												
	Mon.												
4	Tue.	8:00	8:05	8:10	8:15	9:00	9:15	9:50					
	Wed.												
	Thur.	8:00					8:05	9:50					
	Fri.												

(Continued) Sample Schedule for Class Meeting Two Days a Week / 2 Hours Each Day

SCHEDULE FOR CLASS ACTIVITIES

WEEK	DAY	WARMUP	PRETEST				CORRECTIVE PRACTICE		POSTTEST				Rhythm-Development Drills
			TW Attempt 1	TW Attempt 2	Diagnostic Test	Chart	Accuracy and Speed Studies	Skill-Development Paragraphs	TW Attempt 1	TW Attempt 2	Diagnostic Test	Chart	
	Mon.												
5	Tue.	8:00					8:05	8:50	9:05	9:20	9:30	9:45	
	Wed.												
	Thur.	8:00	8:05	8:10	8:15	9:00	9:15	9:50					
	Fri.												
	Mon.												
6	Tue.	8:00					8:05	9:50					
	Wed.												
	Thur.	8:00					8:05	8:50	9:05	9:20	9:30	9:45	
	Fri.												

Corrective practice time per cycle = 3 hours/5 minutes. Four cycles completed. Repeat the schedule for another cycle or two if time permits.

Sample Schedule for Class Meeting Two Days a Week / 2 Hours Each Day

SCHEDULE FOR CLASS ACTIVITIES

WEEK	DAY	WARMUP	PRETEST				CORRECTIVE PRACTICE		POSTTEST				Rhythm-Development Drills
			TW Attempt 1	TW Attempt 2	Diagnostic Test	Chart	Accuracy and Speed Studies	Skill-Development Paragraphs	TW Attempt 1	TW Attempt 2	Diagnostic Test	Chart	
	Mon.												
1	Tue.	8:00	8:05	8:10	8:15	9:00	9:15	9:45					
	Wed.												
	Thur.	8:00					8:05	9:45					
	Fri.												
	Mon.												
2	Tue.	8:00					8:05	9:45					
	Wed.												
	Thur.	8:00					8:05	8:55	9:10	9:20	9:30	9:45	
	Fri.												
	Mon.												
3	Tue.	8:00	8:05	8:10	8:15	9:00	9:15	9:45					
	Wed.												
	Thur.	8:00					8:05	9:45					
	Fri.												
	Mon.												
4	Tue.	8:00					8:05	9:45					
	Wed.												
	Thur.	8:00					8:05	8:55	9:10	9:20	9:30	9:45	
	Fri.												

(Continued) Sample Schedule for Class Meeting Two Days a Week / 2 Hours Each Day

SCHEDULE FOR CLASS ACTIVITIES

WEEK	DAY	WARMUP	PRETEST				CORRECTIVE PRACTICE		POSTTEST				Rhythm-Development Drills
			TW Attempt 1	TW Attempt 2	Diagnostic Test	Chart	Accuracy and Speed Studies	Skill-Development Paragraphs	TW Attempt 1	TW Attempt 2	Diagnostic Test	Chart	
	Mon.												
5	Tue.	8:00	8:05	8:10	8:15	9:00	9:15	9:45					
	Wed.												
	Thur.	8:00					8:05	9:45					
	Fri.												
	Mon.												
6	Tue.	8:00					8:05	9:45					
	Wed.												
	Thur.	8:00					8:05	8:55	9:10	9:20	9:30	9:45	
	Fri.												

Corrective practice time per cycle = 4 hours/40 minutes. Three cycles completed. Repeat the schedule for two or three more cycles if time permits.

Sample Schedule for Class Meeting Five Days a Week / 1 Hour Each Day

SCHEDULE FOR CLASS ACTIVITIES

WEEK	DAY	WARMUP	PRETEST				CORRECTIVE PRACTICE		POSTTEST				Rhythm-Development Drills
			TW Attempt 1	TW Attempt 2	Diagnostic Test	Chart	Accuracy and Speed Studies	Skill-Development Paragraphs	TW Attempt 1	TW Attempt 2	Diagnostic Test	Chart	
1	Mon.	8:00	8:05	8:15	8:30	8:45							
	Tue.	8:00					8:05	8:50					
	Wed.	8:00					8:05	8:50					
	Thur.	8:00					8:05	8:50					
	Fri.	8:00							8:05	8:15	8:30	8:45	
2	Mon.	8:00	8:05	8:15	8:30	8:45							
	Tue.	8:00					8:05	8:50					
	Wed.	8:00					8:05	8:50					
	Thur.	8:00					8:05	8:50					
	Fri.	8:00							8:05	8:15	8:30	8:45	
3	Mon.	8:00	8:05	8:15	8:30	8:45							
	Tue.	8:00					8:05	8:50					
	Wed.	8:00					8:05	8:50					
	Thur.	8:00					8:05	8:50					
	Fri.	8:00							8:05	8:15	8:30	8:45	
4	Mon.	8:00	8:05	8:15	8:30	8:45							
	Tue.	8:00					8:05	8:50					
	Wed.	8:00					8:05	8:50					
	Thur.	8:00					8:05	8:50					
	Fri.	8:00							8:05	8:15	8:30	8:45	

(Continued) Sample Schedule for Class Meeting Five Days a Week / 1 Hour Each Day

SCHEDULE FOR CLASS ACTIVITIES

WEEK	DAY	WARMUP	PRETEST				CORRECTIVE PRACTICE		POSTTEST				Rhythm-Development Drills
			TW Attempt 1	TW Attempt 2	Diagnostic Test	Chart	Accuracy and Speed Studies	Skill-Development Paragraphs	TW Attempt 1	TW Attempt 2	Diagnostic Test	Chart	
5	Mon.	8:00	8:05	8:15	8:30	8:45							
	Tue.	8:00					8:05	8:50					
	Wed.	8:00					8:05	8:50					
	Thur.	8:00					8:05	8:50					
	Fri.	8:00							8:05	8:15	8:30	8:45	
6	Mon.	8:00	8:05	8:15	8:30	8:45							
	Tue.	8:00					8:05	8:50					
	Wed.	8:00					8:05	8:50					
	Thur.	8:00					8:05	8:50					
	Fri.	8:00							8:05	8:15	8:30	8:45	

Corrective practice time per cycle = 2 hours/15 minutes. Six cycles completed.

Helping Your Students Succeed

. . . Through Motivation!!

Cortez Peters, Jr., loved teaching people how to type! . . . and he loved it because *he was successful at it*! His success was achieved because of the way in which he taught. He knew that typing, or keyboarding, could be a tedious and frustrating skill to learn. He also knew that it took a lot of time and a lot of concentration on repetitive drill work for a student to achieve success. The task could be exhausting and boring, and only truly dedicated students would succeed without his intervention. His intervention took the form of motivation . . . and what a great motivator he was! He shares with you these proven strategies that will help ensure your success as a motivator:

1. Be enthusiastic as you explain the practicality and effectiveness of this program's diagnostic/prescriptive approach, diagnosing *individual* problems and prescribing *individualized* corrective practice. Everyone does not have the same kind of keystroking problem! Remind the students that it is this individualized approach that will lead them to keyboarding success!
2. Explain to your students that this program was created by an undefeated typing champion, who was the son of a *world typing champion,* and it is the techniques and strategies that he shares with you that enabled them to become champions!
3. You must be the students' cheerleader, encouraging them to continue even when they think they cannot! Success builds upon success and you must make their success possible:
   - **a.** Be enthusiastic about this program. Display a positive attitude in the effectiveness of the methodology. Show your students that you absolutely believe that if they do what they are supposed to do when they are supposed to do it, they will succeed.

b. Explain to your students that this program will be successful only if they practice and key conscientiously. Remind them that if they only half-try, they will only half-succeed. Since the program probes for weaknesses, those who half-try have to do a tremendous amount of corrective practice. Exhort your students to do their best every day so they will have less corrective practice drills to key.

c. Nurture a positive attitude in your students. Counter their negativity about the repetitiveness of the program with statements about the positive outcomes that result from this repetitiveness!

d. Issue individual certificates for recognition of achievement for Accuracy Honor Roll papers, Speed Honor Roll papers, Super Honor Roll papers, and Excellence in Rhythmic Keystroking.

e. Issue class certificates to recognize improvement in class ending error rate (Championship Keyboarding Class certificate) and to recognize Accuracy, Speed, and Super Honor Roll *Classes* (requirements are explained under item 5 of "Conducting the Class", page 22).

f. Establish a bulletin board to challenge and motivate students. You can:

- Post the goals of the class and display papers that give evidence that goals are being met.
- Display a large poster listing the names and accomplishments of the top keyboarders.
- Post certificates for individual and class achievements.
- Post the achievements of several classes (of your classes as well as other teachers' classes) for comparison. Encourage friendly competition to make the task of keyboarding improvement more interesting and challenging!

4. Radiate genuine concern and interest in each student's keyboarding problems and progress!

a. Hold individual consultation sessions. These sessions begin with the third 5-Minute Timed Writing (second Pretest) and for each timing thereafter whenever a student makes 6 errors or more on a 5-Minute Timed Writing. Hold these sessions during the corrective practice hours. Cortez Peters would place a chair beside his desk and would call on a student to bring all charts and all timed writings to him. He allowed 5 minutes with each student to review the charts. He emphasized Chart 2 (Misstroke Analysis) confirming that the student understood which drills had to be keyed, how they should be keyed, how the computations were made, and how the charting was done. Speak kindly and patiently with each student, offering assurance that with conscientious practice, he or she will indeed improve the following week. Remind the student that conscientious practicing is:

- Reading for duplication, not comprehension.
- Keying on a letter-for-letter basis.
- Saying the letter to himself or herself as he or she keys it.
- Keying with rhythm.
- Looking at the text, not at the keys.

At this student's next consultation, point out improvements that have been noted.

5. Assure the students that you evaluate the corrective practice so they can see that you take this assignment seriously. (See "Corrective Practice" on page 8 for a detailed explanation). If they think you do not take corrective practice seriously enough to grade it, they will not practice conscientiously and will not progress as they should.
6. Let your students know you care. Motivate for performance by rewarding with external rewards such as candy kisses, applause for noteworthy keyboarding success, or a few words of recognition or encouragement. Even a smiley-face sticker on a timed writing will go a long way in winning the cooperation of your students!

If motivation is achieved, there will be few behavior problems. Let them know that you love to teach and that you love people and that their class is going to have a wonderful learning experience!

Conducting the Class

. . . How To Get Started!

The first day of the class is a good time to explain the program, using your motivation techniques. If time allows, you can begin an orientation. The author presents the following suggestions to help you start the program.

1. It will be difficult for the students to succeed if they do not know what they should be doing. Help the students develop a feeling of *ownership* with the program by making sure they understand how the program works.

   a. Review the "Agenda of Cycle Activities", pages 5–7 in the text. Carefully explain the skillbuilding cycle and the charting, making sure the students understand how all of the activities of the cycle fit together. (The charting is a result of the Pretest; corrective practice on Accuracy Studies drills and Speed Studies drills is a result of the charting; the Posttest is to measure the effectiveness of the corrective practice by comparing Posttest results to Pretest results).

   b. Set aside a time (one day or one week, depending on how much time you have) prior to starting the skillbuilding program for *orientation.* If your time is limited, you may actually have to use the first cycle as an orientation. A suggested **Orientation** is presented on pages 26–27 of this manual for your convenience.

   c. Determine the beginning error rate of the class as a whole on its first 5-Minute Timed Writing:

   Step 1. Total the number of errors made by all the students.

   Step 2. Divide this total by the number of students taking the timing.
   Example: Class of 30 students made a total of 660 errors.
   660 ÷ 30 = 22 errors (averaged) per student

2. Explain the philosophy behind the methodology of this program:
   a. Acquiring championship techniques is the first and most important aspect of championship keyboarding.
   b. Concentration is the biggest problem that students will encounter, but they can overcome this problem if they:
      - Read for duplication not comprehension.
      - Type on a letter-by-letter basis.
      - Type with rhythm.
      - Say the letter to themselves as they key it.
      - Do not look at the keys as they type.
   c. Accuracy is always more important than speed.

3. Tell students what you expect of them in order to make this program work:
   a. Follow your instructions.
   b. Practice conscientiously, not nonchalantly.
   c. Key the corrective practice drills (Accuracy Studies and Speed Studies) as directed.

4. Emphasize the importance of accurately recording information on the charts since each student's individual corrective practice drills are prescribed from those recordings.

5. Share with your students your goal(s) for the class:
   a. Your first goal is to reduce the error rate to 3 errors or less on a 5-Minute Timed Writing because accuracy is always the first priority.
   b. Students have an opportunity to achieve *championship* class status—explain how a class can achieve such a status:
      (1) A class can achieve Championship Keyboarding Class status if its ending error rate is 10 errors or more less than its beginning error rate.
      Step 1. Determine the average number of errors per student on each of the last three 5-Minute Timed Writings by following Steps 1 and 2 above under 1(c).
      Step 2. Select the lowest error rate of the three and compare to the beginning error rate.
      Step 3. If the average ending error rate is 10 errors or more less than its average beginning rate, your class qualifies for the Championship Keyboarding Class certificate.
      (2) A class can be an Accuracy Championship Class if it has an average of 5 Accuracy Honor Roll papers per student. For example, a class of 20 students would need 100 honor roll papers during the course of this skillbuilding program.
      (3) A class can be a Speed Championship Class if it has an average of 2 Speed Honor Roll papers per student. For example, a class of 20 students would need a total of 40 speed honor roll papers during the course of this skillbuilding program.

(4) Show the students each of the three individual Honor Roll certificates and review with them the criteria for achieving such a certificate (see page 22 of the text).

(5) Show or tell students about the Certificate for Excellence in Rhythmic Keystroking and let them know how they can earn extra gold stars if they meet certain criteria (page 32 in this manual).

6. Let students know that you are *technique conscious,* and emphasize the importance of mastering championship techniques.

a. Set up a demonstration area, review the techniques, and demonstrate each one. Ask each student to demonstrate the techniques to you either in this demonstration area or at his or her own keyboard.

7. Share with your students how their grades will be determined. You may wish to use all, a combination of, or none of the following suggestions. You may wish to supplement these suggestions or replace them with your own. Factor together the grades from each area for a final grade. (Details of each can be found under the heading "Evaluation", page 33 in this manual):

a. Rhythm-Development Drills—You will factor in only the best grade made during the 3–5 hours of work on the Rhythm-Development Drills.

b. Techniques—You will be observing students' use of the championship techniques during the corrective practice times and will make a subjective evaluation.

c. Corrective Practice—Since corrective practice is essential to accurate keying, you will be evaluating it by considering the number of perfect lines completed.

d. Honor Roll Papers—Honor Roll papers are achievable only after the first 5-Minute Timed Writing, and you will assign a grade based on the number of Honor Roll papers each student achieves.

e. NWAM Improvement—You will issue a grade based on the NWAM improvement from the first 5-Minute Timed Writing to the last 5-Minute Timed Writing.

f. Grade on 5-Minute Timed Writings—You will grade two 5-Minute Timed Writings that the students selected and practiced.

8. Advise your students that they may reach a speed plateau but that there are ways they can overcome it.

a. Speed plateaus on the 5-Minute Timed Writings can be broken by having students select a Rhythm-Development Drill that has a *low* speed that is 5 GWAM *faster* than the fastest speed that they were able to achieve on a 5-Minute Timed Writing. Students should practice this drill for 5 consecutive class hours and should be encouraged to set a goal at keying the drill with zero errors.

b. Speed plateaus on the Skill-Development Paragraphs can be broken by keying each line of the paragraph on a line-by-line basis 10 times, as well as any word on which an error was made or the rhythm was broken 25 times.

Exceptions to the Cycle Procedures

. . . They Are All Subjective!

Throughout this skillbuilding course, situations will arise that will require a decision on your part. A few of these questions, along with corresponding answers, are presented below. Decisions affecting the procedures of the skillbuilding cycle will become easier to make once you have gained experience working with this program.

Q1. Should I ever allow extra corrective practice for a class?

Answer. Yes. Sometimes assembly programs, holidays, and other interruptions shorten the class period or class week. Such interruptions do not allow the students sufficient time in which to do the corrective practice; consequently, they do not make satisfactory progress. If this is the case, you will probably have to extend the cycle's schedule an extra day or so.

Another reason to allow time for extra corrective practice is after you have carefully analyzed the results of the Posttest and found that no progress, or very little progress, was made from the Pretest. If this is the case, you may decide that the students need to spend an extra hour or two on the corrective practice drills prescribed by the next 5-Minute Timed Writing.

Q2. Should I ever exempt a student from taking the second attempt on a 5-Minute Timed Writing?

Answer. Yes. If the student has made any of three Honor Roll papers, you may wish to give him or her the option of skipping the second attempt.

Q3. Should I ever exempt a student or class from taking the cycle's Diagnostic Test?

Answer. Yes. If the results of the Pretest 5-Minute Timed Writing were very poor (a student made 10 or more errors on a Pretest 5-Minute Timed Writing *and* exceeded the number of errors allowed in five or more categories of Chart 2), permit the student to skip the Diagnostic Test for that cycle and, instead, concentrate on keying the Accuracy Studies drills prescribed on Chart 2.

Q4. Should I ever exempt a student from future 5-Minute Timed Writings if his or her current 5-Minute Timed Writing and Diagnostic Test revealed too many errors?

Answer. Yes. If a student made 4 errors or more on five or more of the Diagnostic Test sentences *and* had 10 or more errors on the Pretest 5-Minute Timed Writing *and* exceeded the maximum number of errors allowed in five or more categories of Chart 2, then you should consider exempting that student from further 5-Minute Timed Writings until you see an improvement in accuracy. Assure the student that he or she will be allowed to make up all the 5-Minute Timed Writings and Diagnostic Tests once accuracy is under control. You, the teacher will judge when this will be.

Q5. Can I ever exempt a student from doing the Accuracy Studies as prescribed from Chart 2 and Chart 3?

Answer. Yes. If a student has excellent accuracy (making 3 errors or less on a 5-Minute Timed Writing and having less than 4 errors on eight of the ten Diagnostic Test sentences), you may wish to exempt the student from keying the Accuracy Studies drill as prescribed on Chart 2 and Chart 3 and go directly to the Speed Studies prescribed on Chart 3.

Orientation

. . . to the Skillbuilding Cycle

The following orientation schedule is developed around a class meeting five days a week, 1 hour a day, and using no software or CD-ROM component. Alter this schedule to meet your own course schedule and/or to make allowances in the instructions if you are using the software or CD-ROM components where all computations and charting are conducted by the computer.

On the First Day of Orientation:

1. Have the class take two 5-Minute Timed Writings.
2. Help students to calculate their gross words a minute speed (see "Agenda of Cycle Activities", page 6 in the textbook)
3. Review what constitutes an error (see "Identifying Errors", page 8 in the textbook), and have the students circle all their errors on both 5-Minute Timed Writings.
4. Help students to calculate their net words a minute speed (see "Agenda of Cycle Activities", page 6 in the textbook).
5. Review the criteria for selecting the better of two timed writings (see "Agenda of Cycle Activities", page 6 in the text), and, based on these criteria, have them select the better 5-Minute Timed Writing for charting.

On the Second Day of Orientation:

1. Using the selected 5-Minute Timed Writing, have the students fill in Chart 1 (instructions accompany the chart).
2. Have the students fill in the top part of Chart 2 (instructions accompany the chart).
3. Have the students fill in the bottom part of Chart 2.
4. Walk the students through prioritizing the prescribed Accuracy Studies drills.

On the Third Day of Orientation:

1. Give the students a Diagnostic Test (ten 1-minute timings on specially constructed sentences).
2. Help them determine their gross words a minute (GWAM) speed.
3. Have them determine the number of errors in each sentence, circling each one with 4 or more errors.
4. Instruct the students to fill in Chart 3 (instructions accompany the chart).
5. Walk them through prioritizing the Accuracy Studies and the Speed Studies that are prescribed for corrective practice.

On the Fourth and Fifth Days of Orientation:

1. Have the students to begin keying the corrective practice drills (Accuracy Studies) prescribed on Chart 2 in the sequence they determined. When finished, have them key the corrective practice drills (Accuracy Studies) prescribed on Chart 3 in the sequence they determined. When finished, have them key the corrective practice drills (Speed Studies) prescribed on Chart 3 in the sequence they determined.

   Emphasize that corrective practice drills must be keyed correctly. These drills not only provide extensive practice in keyboarding, they also provide repetitive practice which is *superior* to just extensive practicing. Instructions must be followed exactly and students should practice conscientiously and with concentration.
2. Reserve the last 10–15 minutes of the corrective practice hour, and let the students key the Skill-Development Paragraphs.
3. Once the students have keyed Skill-Development Paragraphs and all the drills that time will allow, have them select several words from the 5-Minute Timed Writings and Diagnostic Test sentences on which they made an error and key those words correctly 25 times. Although this activity should not be introduced until the third 5-Minute Timed Writing has been taken, practicing this during orientation will give the students an idea of how it should be done.

This completes the Orientation in which students actually work through a cycle with your close supervision and instruction.

Problems and Resolutions

. . . What Happens When . .

Q1. The student is unable to finish a particular 1-minute Skill-Development Paragraph or makes too many errors on it.

Answer. Advise the student to key the first line of the paragraph 10 consecutive times and every word on which he or she made an error or broke the rhythm 25 times. Practice each succeeding line similarly. Sometimes this procedure will work the first day, but most likely it will take several days before the student sees success, so you will have to continue to encourage the student to practice conscientiously, because it *will* work!

Q2. The student makes too many errors on the 5-Minute Timed Writings.

Answer. Make sure the student is charting the misstrokes correctly, doing all of the corrective practice drills. Also, make sure the student is keying the drills for each error correctly 25 times. Confirm that the student is keying letter-for-letter. You can also allow the student to work independently on a Rhythm-Development drill that is 5 GWAM slower than the GWAM speed of the latest 5-Minute Timed Writing. Require the student to key the drill with no than 5 errors.

A very poor student may need special treatment. Beginning with the second Pretest, exempt him or her from all 5-Minute Timed Writings and Diagnostic Tests until all of the Accuracy Studies assigned from both Chart 2 and Chart 3 have been completed. Have a consultation session with that student to ensure his or her cooperation. Carefully explain to the student that it is the corrective practice drills that will enable him or her to eliminate accuracy problems. Reassure the student that he or she will be permitted to make up the 5-Minute Timed Writings that were missed. It is vitally important that the poor typing students are given a great deal of individual attention because you want to modify their behavior. You must make certain that your students think and act in a positive manner.

Q3. A student has a negative attitude.

Answer. You can play a major role in the performance level of a student. Your attitude and behavior will significantly impact on the behavior of the class. Be positive and enthusiastic!

Q4. A student can't stop looking at his or her fingers.

Answer. Encourage the student to practice the reaches with which he or she feels insecure. After much practicing, the student should become comfortable with these reaches. You may also have to provide "basketball blinders", available from sporting goods stores or your school's athletic department. The student should wear the blinders while keying corrective practices.

Q5. The student has no speed deficiencies on the Pretest Diagnostic Test.

Answer. Once the student has eliminated all speed deficiencies or has no more than 1 speed deficiency on a Pretest Diagnostic Test, he or she should select the minimum speed goals for each Diagnostic Test sentence from the next speed level when taking the next Diagnostic Test. This assures that the student is being challenged and pushed to achieve higher speeds.

Rhythm-Development Drills

. . . How to Administer Them

Rhythmic typing is one of the most important components—if not *the* most important component—for developing speed and accuracy. Students who type rhythmically type faster and more accurately than other students. Using the Rhythm-Development pacing drills will upgrade the learning process for your students.

The author was exposed to rhythmic typing by his father who, as an old master and world champion typist, was a leading exponent of rhythmic typing. When Cortez Peters, Jr., was learning to type, his father would sit beside him and type at a predetermined pace. Cortez had to type along with his father, matching him stroke for stroke, until he mastered typing at that particular rate of speed. Whenever Cortez reached a speed plateau, his father would repeat the process, but at a faster rate.

To duplicate this pacing technique, the author developed pacing drills against which the students can match their keystroking. Listening to Rhythm-Development tapes, students will learn championship typing rhythm as they key along to the voice and keystrokes of Cortez Peters, Jr., matching him stroke for stroke. Although the drills are for the specific speed rates indicated, the stroking is not necessarily metronomic, so there will be speed variations depending upon the difficulty of the stroke pattern. Nevertheless, the speed rates are reflective of the way Cortez Peters would type a particular word at the designated speed level. As a consequence, the student develops better concentration, better rhythm, better speed, and better accuracy.

Rhythm-Development Drills should be used after the student has completed three full skillbuilding cycles *and* has achieved a speed of 35 gross words a minute on a 5-Minute Timed Writing. The same tape should be used for 3–5 consecutive hours; it can be used longer (but do not exceed a total of 8 hours) if the student's beginning error rate is very high, or until 90 percent of the class can key the entire drill with no more than 5 errors. The drill should be followed by at least one complete skillbuilding cycle, or five cycles if the same drill is to be repeated. As the students practice with the Rhythm-Development Drills, they should be instructed to follow these guidelines:

1. During the first 2 hours of the pacing drills (which are for practice, not evaluation), key 25 times each word on which an error was made; 20 times each phrase on which an error was made; and 10 times each sentence on which an error was made.
2. Audibilize (spell out loud) each stroke in each sentence. If a drill is too fast to audibilize each stroke, then internalize each stroke by spelling it out *mentally.*
3. Practice conscientiously. In order to get the maximum benefit from the drills, students must concentrate totally on what they are keying.

How to Use the Rhythm-Development Drills

There are eight 30-minute drills ranging in speed from 20 WAM to 65 WAM. The drills are available on cassette tapes and accessible in the CD-ROM component. In the CD-ROM component, the script for the drills will be displayed on the screen; in the Rhythm-Development Tape package, the script is provided. The eight drills are as follows:

Tape/Drill 1A = 20, 25, and 30 WAM

Tape/Drill 1B = 25, 30, and 35 WAM

Tape/Drill 2A = 30, 35, and 40 WAM

Tape/Drill 2B = 35, 40, and 45 WAM

Tape/Drill 3A = 40, 45, and 50 WAM

Tape/Drill 3B = 45, 50, and 55 WAM

Tape Drill 4A = 50, 55, and 60 WAM

Tape/Drill 4B = 55, 60, and 65 WAM

If the CD-ROM component is used or if you use the cassette tapes on a multichannel tape player, then each student will be able to select the drill appropriate for his or her own individual speed. However, if you do not have a multichannel tape player, then the class will key the same tape at the same time. Select the drill that has a *top* speed which is at least 5 GWAM *slower* than the slowest GWAM speed of the individual or the slowest GWAM speed in the class. For example, if your class is keying between 40 and 50 GWAM on 5-Minute Timed Writings, and if your whole class will be keying the same tape at the same time, then you would select Tape/ Drill 1B, which has a top speed of 35 WAM—5 WAM slower than the class's slowest speed of 40 WAM.

If you have a student who is keying much slower or much faster than the majority of the students, either allow a separate time for that student to take the drills, provide that student with an individual cassette player and earphones, or use a multiplayer cassette deck so each student, wearing earphones, can select the tape speed that is appropriate for his or her level. To get the best results, the tape must be at least 5

GWAM slower than the student's GWAM speed on his latest 5-Minute Timed Writing. Never use a tape that is equal to or faster than the 5-minute GWAM speed of the student unless that student is trying to break a speed plateau.

Before starting the Rhythm-Development Drills, preview the drills with the students. Let the class key the tape drill for about 5 minutes on the preceding day. This will prepare the class psychologically for rhythmic typing. If your students are not using the software or CD-ROM components, have them:

1. Key their name, date, and drill number at the top of the paper.
2. Space down three lines to begin keying the first line of the drill.
3. Single-space the drill; double-space between each group of sentences.

Earning a Certificate for Achievement

Once the student has earned an ***A*** (see "Rhythm-Development Drills" under the heading "Evaluation", page 35 in this manual), he or she is eligible for the Certificate for Excellence in Rhythmic Keystroking. As a further incentive, gold stars can be affixed to the certificate depending on the number of errors made in the ***A*** range:

For Grades 7–10	*For Grades 11–14*
0 errors = 3 gold stars	0 errors = 3 gold stars
1–4 errors = 2 gold stars	1–2 errors = 2 gold stars
5–8 errors = 1 gold star	3–5 errors = 1 gold star
9–10 errors = certificate	5 errors = certificate

Students who have earned 2 gold stars are eligible for an additional star only when they are able to type the same tape drill perfectly—that is, with no errors. These awards can be presented at the end of the skill-building cycle, at the end of the tape drill, or at the end of the course.

Using the Drills to Break Speed Plateaus

If the student has reached a speed plateau, try to increase his speed by selecting a drill which has a low speed that is 5 GWAM *faster* than the speed the student is able to achieve on a 5-Minute Timed Writing. The student should practice with this tape for 3–5 consecutive hours. The goal is to key the tape with zero errors before moving on to the next tape.

However, as the student increases in speed, he or she will probably notice a corresponding increase in errors. If this occurs, instruct the student to take a 5-Minute Timed Writing pushing for a speed that is 5 GWAM faster than the speed plateau rate. The student should then record the results on Chart 2 and practice the accuracy drills as prescribed. To continue gaining speed, the student should always select, and push to keep pace with, a rate that is 5 GWAM faster than the last 5-Minute Timed Writing speed.

... / N° DU CONTRÔLE MHR	CUST. ORDER NO. / N° DE COMM.	FOB MHR WAREHOUSE / FAB ENTREPÔT MHR	CUSTOMER NO. / N° DU CLIENT
BO1364604	C. SMITH		014719991

QTY / QTÉ	ISBN	TRN	ED. NO.	AUTHOR / AUTEUR P.O. / BON D'ACHAT — TITLE / TITRE LOCATION / ENDROIT	R	PRICE / PRIX	DISC. ESC.	NET EXTENDED PRICE PRIX NET	TAXE
				************************************					
				*** COMPLIMENTARY / COMPLIMENTAIRE **					
				************************************					
1	0028012011	68	03	CORTEZ PE IMK CHAMP KEYBDG DRILLS	1		100	0.00	
				* PICK LOC: 44 26 012 1 QTY: 1					
1	0028012062	68	03	CORTEZ PE CHAMP KEYBD DRILLS DEMO DISK	1		100	0.00	
				* PICK LOC: 22 35 102 1 QTY: 1					
				COMPLIMENTS OF ANITA WILKES					
				PHONE: (800) 261-0199					
				E-MAIL: anitaw@mcgrawhill.ca					
				VISIT US AT WWW.MCGRAWHILL.CA					

SPECIAL INSTRUCTIONS / INSTRUCTIONS SPÉCIALES

0000 (INV) * PIECE KILO

MESSAGES

WOG CODE: 0 DO NOT HOLD

METHOD OF PAYMENT / MODE DE PAIEMENT

CHARGE ACCOUNT # / N° DE COMPTE

EXPIRY DATE / DATE D'EXPIRATION

AUTHORIZATION NO. / N° D'AUTORISATION

WEIGHT / POIDS: 0.8LBS

TERMS / TERMES

SUB-TOTAL / TOTAL PARTIEL		0.00
GST APPLICABLE ON / TPS APPLICABLE SUR	0.00	0.00
TRANS/HANDLING / TRANSPORT ET MANUTENTION		0.00
GST ON TRANS/HANDLING / TPS SUR TRANSPORT ET MANUTENTION		0.00
PST APPLICABLE ON / TVP APPLICABLE SUR	0.00	0.00
TOTAL ▶		0.00

LEGEND / LÉGENDE

- NYP - Not yet published - Sous presse - sera expédié après publication
- NOP - Not our publication - Pas une publication MHR
- TOS - Temporarily out of stock cancelled - Quantité temporairement épuisée - annulée
- NTR - No trade rights - cancelled - MHR ne possède pas les droits - annulée
- RFR - Restricted foreign rights - Droits d'auteur à l'étranger limités
- OP - Out of print - Édition épuisée
- PC - Publication cancelled - Publication annulée
- PD - Publication delayed - order cancelled - Publication différée - commande annulée
- OS - Out of stock-back ordered - Stock épuisé-articles en souffrance

CLAIMS FOR SHORTAGES OR DAMAGE MUST BE MADE UPON RECEIPT OF GOODS. BOOKS WHICH HAVE BEEN MARKED OR STAMPED MAY NOT BE RETURNED./ LES RÉCLAMATIONS POUR LIVRES MANQUANTS OU ABÎMES DOIVENT ÊTRE SOUMISES IMMÉDIATEMENT. TOUT LIVRE MARQUÉ OU ESTAMPILLÉ NE POURRA PLUS ÊTRE RETOURNÉ.

ORDS REV. 1/96

B013644604 SMITH 014719991

****

*** COMPLIMENTARY / COMPLIMENTAIRE **

****

I 0028012011168	03CORTEZ PE IMK CHAMP KEYBDG DRILLS	1	100		0.00
	* PICK LOC: 44 26 012 1 QTY: 1				
I 0028012062668	03CORTEZ PE CHAMP KEYBD DRILLS DEMO DISKI		100		0.00
	* PICK LOC: 22 35 102 1 QTY: 1				

COMPLIMENTS OF ANITA WILKES
PHONE: (800) 261-0199
E-MAIL: anitaw@mcgrawhill.ca
VISIT US AT WWW.MCGRAWHILL.CA

0000 (INV) * PIECE KILO	0.8LBS			0.00
			0.00	0.00
				0.00
WOG CODE: 0 DO NOT HOLD				0.00
			0.00	0.00
				0.00

Evaluation

. . . *Grading Suggestions and Guidelines*

Since you will need to evaluate the progress of each student, the author has suggested six areas that could be used for assigning a grade. The six areas are as follows: corrective practice, techniques, number of Honor Roll papers, Rhythm-Development Drills, NWAM improvement, and the grade on two 5-Minute Timed Writings. You may have to modify the grading standards because of the age of your students, their mental and physical capabilities, or because of other factors that will impact their performance. Some of the areas, such as *techniques,* will require your *subjective* judgment in evaluating the performance level. You can determine a student's final grade for the skillbuilding course by averaging the final grades from each of the areas. You may wish to supplement these suggested areas or adapt them to reflect your own grading needs. It is a good idea to share with your students the areas in which they will be graded and how you will arrive at a grade for each of the areas.

Corrective Practice (20%)

To ensure that you get the proper student behavior, you should grade the corrective practice drills. Otherwise, your students will quickly lose interest in producing quality work, and if this occurs, you will find that your students will not improve their accuracy. Typing practice is only meaningful when students practice conscientiously, and they will not practice conscientiously if they think you are not looking at their work.

It is not necessary to grade all of the corrective practice drills; choose randomly selected pages. Once during each cycle, ask the students to staple their corrective practice work together and turn it in for grading. Select two pages of the work and check to make sure that the required

number of perfect lines (for the drills that were actually completed) were keyed. Make a copy of the **Corrective Practice Grade Chart** on page 40. Total the number of deficiencies in perfect lines for each drill line keyed. If a student was to key 3 perfect lines of a particular drill, but keyed only 2 perfect lines, the deficiency would be 1. Mark that group of lines with a **–1** (minus 1). Total the number of deficient lines and compute a grade accordingly. Record the grade under the appropriate cycle number.

If a student's accuracy is very poor and a great many drills have been prescribed as a result, then it will probably require quite a bit of time on that student's part to achieve the number of perfect lines required by each drill. In this case, it is unlikely that the student will be able to complete all of the assignments. Therefore, in addition to checking the number of perfect lines, you may wish to consider the number of drills completed *in relation to* the number that had been prescribed. You will have to adapt the grading scale to your satisfaction in order to accommodate this criteria.

–1 = A
–2 through –4 = B
–5 through –7 = C
–8 and –9 = D
–10 or more = F

Techniques (20%)

During the corrective practice hours, observe each student to see if he or she is using the keystroking and positioning techniques and rhythmic keystroking techniques as discussed in the text (page viii) under the heading "Championship Techniques." Hopefully, as suggested, you set up a demonstration area and demonstrated these various techniques and emphasized the importance of acquiring them. This will be a subjective evaluation on your part. Make a copy of the **Technique Evaluation Chart** (see page 41 in this manual), and for each student, record a grade to reflect your observations. Average this grade in with the grades of the other areas to arrive at a final grade for this skill-building course.

Number of Honor Roll Papers (20%)

Honor Roll papers are a result of keying a 5-Minute Timed Writing with no more than 1 error, and they reveal a relationship between accuracy and speed. There are three types of Honor Roll papers: Accuracy Honor Roll, Speed Honor Roll, and Super Honor Roll. Each of these is described on page 22 of the text. You can assign a grade based on the number of Honor Roll papers in relation to the number of 5-Minute Timed Writings taken. For example, if the student keyed eight or more Honor Roll papers out of fifteen 5-Minute Timed Writings taken, then he or she would receive an ***A***. However, if he keyed 8 out of 25, then he

might receive a ***B*** or even a ***C***. The following grades are based on fifteen 5-Minute Timed Writings. Adjust the grading scale if your students take more than or fewer than fifteen timed writings.

8 or more	= A
6 – 7	= B
4 – 5	= C
2 – 3	= D
1 or less	= F

Rhythm-Development Drills (15%)

Your goal is to have the students key a drill and make 5 errors or less. Each drill (1A, 1B, etc.) requires approximately 30 minutes to complete. Grades are based on the number of errors made each time through the drill. Use a copy of the Rhythm-Development Drill Chart on page 42 to record a student's progress. For example, the first time a student completes Drill 1A, you would record the number of errors made under "first" for Drill 1A. The second time the student goes through the tape drill, you would record the number of errors made under "second" for Drill 1A. Since the first two attempts through each drill are only "practice," you should not figure the number of errors made during these first two attempts into the final grade for the drill. You would use only the number of errors recorded for the third, fourth, and fifth times (or sixth, seventh, or eighth times if additional time was needed) through the drill to compute a student's final grade for that particular drill number. Once you have added the number of errors made for the third, fourth, and fifth times through a particular drill, you can equate a grade. The following drill grades are based on the total number of errors made for the third, fourth, and fifth tries on the drill. If an additional three times are needed to practice the drills because the accuracy is so poor, use the number of errors made on only the last three (sixth, seventh, and eighth) times through the drill to figure the final grade for that particular drill.

For Grades 7–10:	*For Grades 11–14:*
1–10 errors = A	1– 5 errors = A
11–20 errors = B	6–10 errors = B
21–30 errors = C	11–15 errors = C
31–40 errors = D	16–20 errors = D
41+ errors = F	21+ errors = F

Sample Grading Chart

Name ______________ Class ______________ Grade ______________

CORTEZ PETERS'
RHYTHM-DEVELOPMENT DRILL CHART

This chart will reflect the performance of your students each time they key a drill. The first time they key a particular drill, record the number of errors made under "1st Time." The second time they key the drill, record the number of errors made under "2nd Time," and so forth. The same tape/drill should be used for 5 consecutive class hours (longer if their beginning error rate is very high but not to exceed eight hours total) or until 90% of your class can key an entire tape drill with 5 errors or less. Your goal is to have the students key the entire drill with 5 errors or less.

	SUGGESTED LENGTH OF USE					ADDITIONAL DAYS IF NEEDED			
	Practice Days		Evaluation Days*			Evaluation Days			
DRILLS	1st Time	2nd Time	3rd Time	4th Time	5th Time	6th Time	7th Time	8th Time	GRADE
1A	33	28	21	17	13	9	5	3	D
1B	21	15	9	5	1				C
2A	14	11	5	2	0				B
2B	12	9	3	1	0				A
3A									
3B									
4A									

*These become *practice days* and are not figured into the final tape grade if the three additional days are used. If the three additional days are used, it is the number of errors made during these last three days that is used to determine the final grade for the tape drill.

NWAM Improvement (15%)

This grading component is based on the improvement in the NWAM speed from the first 5-Minute Timed Writing to the last.

20 or more NWAM = A
15 – 19 NWAM = B
10 – 14 NWAM = C
5 – 9 NWAM = D
0 – 4 NWAM = F

Note: This grading component will be satisfactory for students typing between 20 and 40 *gross* words a minute; however, when students type faster, it becomes increasingly difficult to increase the NWAM speed by 20 WAM over a five- or six-week period. For a student keying 100 WAM, an increase of just 5 WAM in a six-week period would be, because of the level, an ***A.***

Grade on Two 5-Minute Timed Writings (10%)

Students will be graded on two **different** 5-Minute Timed Writings that contain no more than 3 errors and are equal to or greater than the GWAM speed of that student's latest 5-Minute Timed Writing. You or the student should determine the two timings that are to be keyed. The student may practice the timing as many times as he or she wants before taking the timing, and the student may take the timing as many times he or she wants in order to achieve the desired grade.

3 errors or less = A
4 errors = B
5 errors = C
6 errors = D
more than 6 = F

The preceding evaluations can be recorded on the **Grade Summary Chart** that is on page 43 of this manual.

CHARTS

The following charts are provided for your convenience and may be duplicated for use with the *Cortez Peters' Championship Keyboarding Drills* program.

CORRECTIVE PRACTICE GRADE CHART

Name	CYCLES														
	1	2	3	4	5	6	7	8	9	10	11	12	13	14	Average

Beside each student's name record a grade that reflects his or her performance on the corrective practice drills. Refer to the "Corrective Practice" heading on page 33 of this instructor's manual for grading instructions.

TECHNIQUE EVALUATION CHART FOR CYCLE ______

Name	TECHNIQUES																			
	Body	Posture	Feet	Wrists	Hands	Palms	Arms	Eyes	Thumbs	Rhy.-Dev. Tapes	Body	Posture	Feet	Wrists	Hands	Palms	Arms	Eyes	Thumbs	Rhy.-Dev. Tapes

Review techniques twice each cycle during corrective practice. Record a grade based on your subjective evaluation of each student's application of championship techniques.

A = Excellent application B = Good application C = Fair application D = Poor application F = Unsatisfactory application

GRADING CHART

Name ______________________ Class ______________________ Grade ______________________

CORTEZ PETERS' RHYTHM-DEVELOPMENT DRILL CHART

This chart will reflect the performance of your students each time they key a drill. The first time they key a particular drill, record the number of errors made under "1st Time." The second time they key the drill, record the number of errors made under "2nd Time," and so forth. The same tape/drill should be used for 5 consecutive class hours (longer if their beginning error rate is very high but not to exceed eight hours total) or until 90% of your class can key an entire tape drill with 5 errors or less. Your goal is to have the students key the entire drill with 5 errors or less.

	SUGGESTED LENGTH OF USE					ADDITIONAL DAYS IF NEEDED			
	Practice Days		Evaluation Days*			Evaluation Days			
DRILLS	1st Time	2nd Time	3rd Time	4th Time	5th Time	6th Time	7th Time	8th Time	GRADE
1A									
1B									
2A									
2B									
3A									
3B									
4A									
4B									

*These become *practice days* and are not figured into the final tape grade if the three additional days are used. If the three additional days are used, it is the number of errors made during these last three days that is used to determine the final grade for the tape drill.

GRADE SUMMARY CHART

Name	Corrective Practice (20%)	Techniques (20%)	Number of Honor Roll Papers (20%)		Rhythm-Dev. Drills (15%)	NWAM Improvement (15%)	Two 5-Minute Timed Writings (10%)		Other (%)	Final Grade
			Accuracy (10%)	Speed (10%)			TW #___	TW #___		

If you add another area in **Other** column, be sure to adjust the percentages to accommodate this additional area.

SCHEDULE FOR CLASS ACTIVITIES

WEEK	DAY	WARMUP	PRETEST				CORRECTIVE PRACTICE		POSTTEST				Rhythm-Development Drills
			TW Attempt 1	TW Attempt 2	Diagnostic Test	Chart	Accuracy and Speed Studies	Skill-Development Paragraphs	TW Attempt 1	TW Attempt 2	Diagnostic Test	Chart	
	Mon.												
	Tue.												
	Wed.												
	Thur.												
	Fri.												
	Mon.												
	Tue.												
	Wed.												
	Thur.												
	Fri.												
	Mon.												
	Tue.												
	Wed.												
	Thur.												
	Fri.												
	Mon.												
	Tue.												
	Wed.												
	Thur.												
	Fri.												
	Mon.												
	Tue.												
	Wed.												
	Thur.												
	Fri.												

(continued)

SCHEDULE FOR CLASS ACTIVITIES

WEEK	DAY	WARMUP	PRETEST				CORRECTIVE PRACTICE		POSTTEST				Rhythm-Development Drills
			TW Attempt 1	TW Attempt 2	Diagnostic Test	Chart	Accuracy and Speed Studies	Skill-Development Paragraphs	TW Attempt 1	TW Attempt 2	Diagnostic Test	Chart	
	Mon.												
	Tue.												
	Wed.												
	Thur.												
	Fri.												
	Mon.												
	Tue.												
	Wed.												
	Thur.												
	Fri.												
	Mon.												
	Tue.												
	Wed.												
	Thur.												
	Fri.												

If the Rhythm-Development Tapes are used to increase speed and accuracy through rhythmic keystroking, you should introduce them as soon as the student has completed three full skillbuilding cycles and has achieved a 35 GWAM speed on a 5-Minute Timed Writing. Each drill should be used for 5 consecutive hours and should be *followed* by at least one full skillbuilding cycle. Directions for using the Rhythm-Development Drills are on page 30 of this manual under the heading *"RHYTHM DEVELOPMENT DRILLS."* Identify the first week that you begin this skillbuilding program as Week 1. Locate the first meeting day of the week and schedule the cycle activities that your class will be performing that day by recording the starting times for each activity. Repeat this process for the second meeting day of the week. Repeat this scheduling procedure for each week, following the recommended time allowances and guidelines on page 11 of this manual.

Certificates

The following seven certificates are provided for your convenience and may be duplicated for use with the *Cortez Peters' Championship Keyboarding Drills* program.

Accuracy Honor Roll

This is to certify that

____

has earned the distinction of achieving the Accuracy Honor Roll.

__________ Net Words a Minute

__________ Number of Errors

__________ Gross Words a Minute

__________ Date of Test

____
Instructor

____
Date

Speed Honor Roll

This is to certify that

____

has earned the distinction of achieving the Speed Honor Roll.

__________ Net Words a Minute

__________ Number of Errors

__________ Gross Words a Minute

__________ Date of Test

____
Instructor

____
Date

EXCELLENCE

Super Honor Roll

This is to certify that

____

has earned the distinction of achieving the Super Honor Roll by displaying championship speed and accuracy.

__________ Net Words a Minute

__________ Number of Errors

__________ Gross Words a Minute

__________ Date of Test

____

Instructor

____

Date

EXCELLENCE

Cortez Peters'

Certificate For Excellence in Rhythmic Keystroking

This certifies that

____

has demonstrated excellence in rhythmic keystroking while maintaining a high degree of accuracy.

____________________________ ____________________________

Instructor | Date Awarded

Accuracy Championship Keyboarding Class

It is with great pride that this certificate is presented to

____

as a member of an Accuracy Championship Keyboarding Class. This class has demonstrated a high degree of accuracy development and has successfully averaged five Accuracy Honor Roll papers per student on 5-Minute Timed Writings.

____
Date Awarded

____
School

____
Instructor

Speed Championship Keyboarding Class

It is with great pride that this certificate is presented to

____

as a member of a Speed Championship Keyboarding Class. This class has demonstrated a high degree of speed development and has successfully averaged two Speed Honor Roll papers per student on 5-Minute Timed Writings.

____
Date Awarded

____
School

____
Instructor

Championship Keyboarding Class

This is to certify that

____

is a member of a Championship Keyboarding Class. This class has demonstrated a high degree of accuracy development by successfully reducing its error rate by a minimum of 10 words on a 5-Minute Timed Writing. In recognition of this extraordinary skill development feat, this certificate is proudly presented.

____________________ Date Awarded

____________________ School

____________________ Instructor

1937 World Championship International Typewriting Contest Rules

The following contest rules reflect the standards for typing contests in 1937. They have been included here as something of interest to share with your students.

GENERAL RULES: Every word omitted, inserted, misspelled, transposed, or in any manner changed from the printed copy and rewritten matter, shall be penalized.

PENALTY: Ten (10) words shall be deducted from the gross number of words for each error.

ONE ERROR ONLY shall be penalized in a word. Should an error occur in the printed copy it may be corrected or written as per copy.

SPACES AND PUNCTUATION MARKS shall be treated as part of the preceding word.

CUT CHARACTERS: Any word written so close to the top, bottom or sides of the sheet that a portion of any letter is cut off, shall be penalized.

DIVISION OF WORDS: A word incorrectly divided at the end of the line shall be penalized.

FAULTY SHIFTING AND LIGHTLY STRUCK LETTERS: An error shall be charged if the complete character is not discernible.

TRANSPOSITIONS: Transposed letters constitute an error. Transposed words are penalized one error for the transposition plus additional penalty if other errors occur.

IN REWRITTEN MATTER: Every word containing an error shall be penalized whether in the first or second writing, and one additional error charged for the rewriting. Strokes in rewritten matter are not counted in the gross.

PILING: If any portion of one character overlaps any portion of another character or extends into the space between words to the extent that it would overlap any portion of a character in that space, it is an error.

UNIFORM LEFT-HAND MARGIN and indentation for paragraphs shall be observed. An error shall be charged for each violation.

LENGTH OF PAGE: With paper 8½" × 13", each page except the last, shall have at least 35 lines of writing. With paper 8½" × 11", each page except the last shall have at least 29 lines of writing. One error is charged for each short page except the last page.

LINE SPACING: Straight copy work shall be doublespaced (2) notches. For every line singly or irregularly spaced one (1) error shall be charged.

PARAGRAPHING: Paragraphs shall be indented five (5) spaces, and only five.

LENGTH OF LINE: Except at the end of a paragraph a line having fewer than sixty-one (61) or more than seventy-six (76) characters and spaces shall be penalized one error.

All copies shall be considered as having been written in one continuous line.

Should the last character on a line be a letter occupying the sixtieth space, there is no error for a short line; however, should the last character on a line be a letter occupying the seventy-sixth space, an error shall be charged for a long line.

In the event any contestant completes the copy, he must continue writing at the beginning of the copy, and in such cases two (2) strokes shall be added to the total shown at the end of the copy.

Anything not described in these rules and any questions as to the interpretation of the rules shall be subject to the decision of the contest Manager. Such decisions shall be final.

Software Information

. . . Using the Software or CD-ROM Components

The last section of this manual is the User Guide that accompanies all software components. It is included in here for your convenience. The User Guide provides complete installation instructions as well as instructions for using the software to implement the *Cortez Peters' Championship Keyboarding Drills* program.

Cortez Peters' Championship Keyboarding Drills Software

User's Guide

Windows 3.1 Version

Glencoe Customer Software Support

Thank you for purchasing this Glencoe software product. Glencoe is dedicated to providing you with the highest quality software and ensuring that you receive the finest technical support for products you purchase. Telephone support for all registered users is available between 8:30 A.M. and 4:00 P.M. (ET) at 1-800-437-3715.

If you have any questions regarding our customer support policy, please write to us at this address:

Glencoe/McGraw-Hill
ATTN: Software Support Center
936 Eastwind Drive
Westerville, OH 43081

This document has been prepared with the assistance of Dolphin Inc., Gibbsboro, NJ.

Contents

Chapter 4: Types of Exercises

Appendix: Troubleshooting Guide

Index

Chapter 1: Welcome

Welcome to the *Cortez Peters' Championship Keyboarding Drills Software* (CP3), an individualized diagnostic and prescriptive method for developing accuracy and speed at the keyboard. CP3 is a Windows-based program designed for use with the *Cortez Peters' Championship Keyboarding Drills* textbook. The student keys exercises from the textbook or screen, and the software scores and charts the student's performance, diagnoses weaknesses, and prescribes corrective practice.

The student's work is stored on a floppy data disk or in a hard-disk directory. Printouts of scores, scored copy, and charts are available at all times. Special Instructor Options allow you to control certain settings for students' use of the software.

CP3 represents a proven concept in developing speed and accuracy at the keyboard and was developed by Cortez Peters, Jr., who, like his father, was a championship typist. The philosophy that shapes this program is derived from the author's own experience and his World Championship Typewriting background. Cortez Peters, Jr., shares with you here the techniques, methods, and strategies that enabled him and his father to become world championship typists. Who better to learn from than world championship typists!

CP3 is flexible to meet your unique requirements. You can have students use the structured, cycle approach (as Cortez Peters recommends), or you can have students follow a sequence that you define. Either way, CP3 gives you all the tools you need to help your students build speed and accuracy.

- The structured approach is a cycle that begins with a Pretest (consisting of a 5-Minute Timed Writing and a Diagnostic Test) to diagnose problem areas. The Pretest is followed by corrective practice and concludes with a Posttest to assess gains in speed and/or accuracy. The top row of the Main Menu should be used to follow the cycle approach. You can supplement the activities of the cycle with Supplemental 5-Minute Timed Writings and Diagnostic Tests available from the bottom row of the Main Menu. Refer to your text ("Agenda of Cycle Activities:" and "Cycle Instructions") for an overview of the activities your students will be doing.

- To use an unstructured approach, you simply have students use the bottom row of the Main Menu and select activities in the sequence that you prefer.

About this User's Guide

This User's Guide provides the information you need to install and operate the CP3 software.

- Chapter 1 provides an overview of this software and preparation for its use.
- Chapter 2 explains the installation and set-up procedures.
- Chapter 3 explains the start-up procedure and provides general navigation and operating instructions.
- Chapter 4 describes in detail each type of exercise included in CP3.
- The Appendix is a Troubleshooting Guide, which lists common problems and suggested solutions.
- The Index provides a quick way to look up specific information in this User's Guide.

For more information about the Cortez Peters philosophy, the recommended cycle approach, or background information on the charting done in CP3, refer to the text or Instructor's Manual.

Package Contents

There are two versions of the *Cortez Peters' Championship Keyboarding Drills Software*: a floppy-disk version and a CD-ROM version. The floppy-disk version includes all exercises in the textbook, but no Cortez Peters video clips or audio for the Cortez Peters Rhythm Development tape drills. The CD-ROM version includes all exercises in the textbook plus numerous Cortez Peters video clips as well as audio for the Cortez Peters Rhythm Development tape drills.

Floppy-Disk Package

The floppy-disk version of the Instructor's CP3 package includes these components:

- Two 3 1/2" program disks.
- One 3 1/2" student data disk for storing student work.

- This User's Guide.
- Site License.

CD-ROM Package The CD-ROM version of the Instructor's CP3 package includes these components:

- The CP3 CD-ROM disc.
- A 3 1/2" student data disk for storing student work.
- This User's Guide.
- Site License.

System Requirements

To run CP3, your system must meet the following minimum requirements:

- IBM or compatible PC with a 80486 or Pentium CPU.
- 8MB RAM.
- Hard disk with 7MB of free space.
- High-density 3 1/2" floppy disk drive or CD-ROM drive.
- sVGA or higher graphics adapter set to 256 colors and Small Fonts mode (640 x 480).
- DOS 5.0 or higher.
- Microsoft Windows 3.1 or Windows 95 (running as a Window 3.1 application).
- Microsoft-compatible mouse.
- A printer is recommended but not required.

Preparation for Using the Software

Before using the CP3 software, do the following:

1. If you are going to install the software from floppy disks, make back-up copies of all CP3 diskettes. Store the original diskettes in a safe place and use your back-up copies for installing the program. See your Windows user's guide if you don't know how to make copies of diskettes.

2. Install CP3 on a hard drive or network drive. See "Installation," pages 5-9.

3. If you want all of your students to store their work on a local or network hard-disk drive, set up student data files. See "Setting Up Student Data Files," pages 9-10.

4. Start up CP3 and access Program Options. Then create an options file for your students to use. See "Setting Program Options," pages 10-13.

Chapter 2: Installation and Set-Up

Installation

For both floppy-disk and CD-ROM versions of CP3, you must install the software before you can run it. The installer sets up a new program group and program icon for CP3 and, for the floppy-disk version, copies files to a directory on your hard disk (the CD-ROM version is run directly from the CD-ROM disc).

Floppy-Disk Installation

Here is the procedure for installing the floppy-disk version of CP3 on a stand-alone computer (see "Network Installation," pages 8-9 if you want to install CP3 on a network).

1. Make sure that the hard disk or network drive where you want to install CP3 has sufficient space. CP3 requires 7MB of free space.
2. Turn on your computer and get into Windows.
3. Insert the CP3 Program Disk 1 into your floppy drive.
4. At the Windows Program Manager, choose *Run* from the File menu.
5. In the Command Line blank, key **a:\install** (where "a:" represents the floppy disk drive). Click OK. See Figure 2-1.

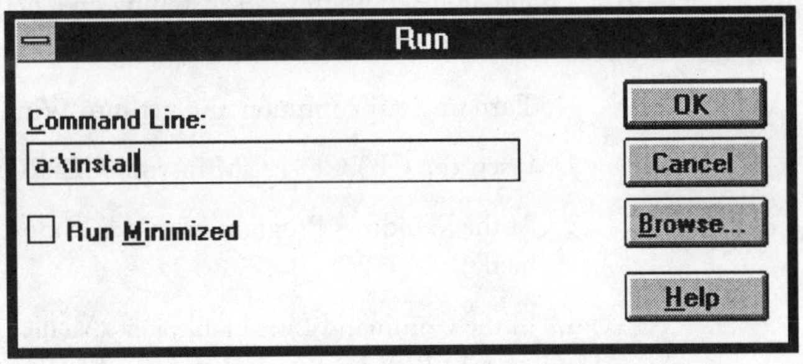

FIGURE 2-1: RUN DIALOG BOX

6. The installer lists your hard disks: select the hard disk where you want to install the program and click **OK**.
7. Next, the installer lists a default directory for the program (\CP3): click **OK** to accept the default, or key a different path and click **OK**.

8. The installer now copies program files onto your hard disk. Switch disks when the installer prompts you to do so.

9. A dialog box asks you where the student will store CP3 work.
   - Select **Store data on data disk A** if the student will store work on a CP3 data disk in floppy disk drive A.
   - Select **Store data on data disk B** if the student will store work on a CP3 data disk in floppy disk drive B.
   - Select **Store data on hard disk drive** if the student will store work in a data directory on the local or network hard-disk drive.

   Click **OK** to continue.

10. If you selected **Store data on hard disk drive** in step 9, above, two dialog boxes ask you where you want to store data files. Choose a drive and click **OK**, then type a directory name and click **OK**.

11. A dialog box tells you that set-up is complete. Click **OK**. You are now back at the Program Manager, with your new Cortez Peters Keyboarding program icon selected on your desktop.

❖ **Note:** If you specified that student data would be stored on the hard-disk drive, one student data directory is created. If you want other students to store their work in data directories, you will need to set up data directories and program icons for each additional student. See "Setting Up Student Data Files," pages 9-10.

CD-ROM Set-Up

Here is the procedure for installing the CD-ROM version of CP3 on a stand-alone computer (for installing on a network, see "Network Installation," pages 8-9).

1. Turn on your computer and get into Windows.
2. Insert the CP3 CD-ROM in your CD-ROM drive.
3. At the Windows Program Manager, choose *Run* from the File menu.
4. In the Command Line blank, key **x:\setup** (where "x:" represents the CD-ROM drive). Click **OK**. See Figure 2-2.

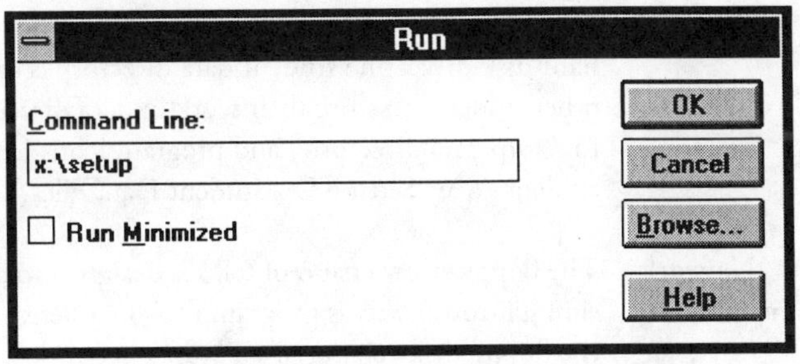

FIGURE 2-2: RUN DIALOG BOX

5. A dialog box asks you where the student will store CP3 work.
   - Select **Store data on data disk A** if the student will store work on a CP3 data disk in floppy disk drive A.
   - Select **Store data on data disk B** if the student will store work on a CP3 data disk in floppy disk drive B.
   - Select **Store data on hard disk drive** if the student will store work in a data directory on the local or network hard-disk drive.

   Click **OK** to continue.

6. If you selected **Store data on hard disk drive** in step 5, above, two dialog boxes ask you where you want to store data files. Choose a drive and click **OK**, then type a directory and click **OK**.

7. A dialog box tells you that set-up is complete. Click **OK**. You are now back at the Program Manager.

8. Check to see if the computer has Microsoft Video for Windows installed.
   - Double-click on the Control Panel icon (generally found in the Main program group).
   - Double-click on the Drivers icon in the Control Panel group.
   - Scroll through the drivers list to find "Microsoft Video for Windows" (or "[MIC] Microsoft Video for Windows"). Click **Cancel** to exit the drivers dialog box and then close the Control Panel program group.

9. If Microsoft Video for Windows is not listed in your drivers (step 8, above), install Microsoft Video for Windows now. To do so, double-click on the VfW Setup icon in the Glencoe Keyboarding program group and follow the on-screen prompts. Restart your computer after you have installed Microsoft Video for Windows.

❖ **Note:** If you specified that student data would be stored on the hard-disk drive, one student data directory is created. If you want other students to store their work in data directories, you will need to set up data directories and program icons for each additional student. See "Setting Up Student Data Files," pages 9-10.

Network Installation

The floppy-disk version of CP3 is designed to allow multiple users to simultaneously access program files on a network drive. To install the floppy-disk version of CP3 on a network:

1. Follow the procedure outlined in "Floppy-Disk Installation," pages 5-6, specifying a network drive instead of a stand-alone hard-disk drive.

2. If you want to have students store their work in data directories on the network, rather than on CP3 data disks, set up student data directories and CP3 program icons (see "Setting Up Student Data Files," pages 9-10). Make sure that each student has read and write access to his or her data directory.

❖ **Note:** Check with your LAN administrator to determine how to verify or grant access rights on your network.

3. Verify that students have read access to the CP3 directory on the network drive (or whatever name you used for the directory where you installed CP3).

4. Verify that you have read and write access to the CP3 directory on the network drive (or whatever name you used for the directory where you installed CP3).

The CD-ROM version of CP3 includes a set-up program, which creates a program group and icon for CP3 but does not install the CP3 program files to a hard-disk drive. If you set up the CD-ROM version of CP3 to run on a networked CD-ROM drive, the video may run very slowly according to the speed of your LAN. For this reason, it is recommended that the CD-ROM not be networked but, instead, used on a stand-alone computer. However, if you choose to use the CD-ROM version and want your students to access CP3 on a networked CD-ROM drive:

1. Follow the procedure outlined in "CD-ROM Set-Up," pages 6-7. The CD-ROM disk must be left in the CD-ROM drive of the network server so the videos can be accessed.

2. If you want to have students store their work in data directories on a network drive, rather than on CP3 data disks, set up student

data directories and CP3 program icons (see "Setting Up Student Data Files," pages 9-10). Make sure that each student has read and write access to his or her data directory.

3. Verify that you and students have access to the CD-ROM drive that holds the CD-ROM disk.
4. Start up CP3 and access Program Options to verify that the Standard options file is what you want your students to use (see "Setting Program Options," pages 10-13). If you modify the Standard options file or create a new options file, you will need to copy the CP3OPTS subdirectory in your WINDOWS directory to the WINDOWS directory on each workstation that will access CP3. The CP3OPTS subdirectory is where options files are stored. (If your students use the Standard options file with its default settings, there is no need to copy the CP3OPTS subdirectory to workstations.)

Installation Problems

If you have any questions or problems as you install CP3, first make sure that your system meets the requirements outlined in "System Requirements," page 3, and that you followed the exact procedure outlined above. Next, refer to the Troubleshooting Guide (Appendix) for solutions to common problems. If you still cannot install the software, record exactly where you were when you encountered the problem. Then call Glencoe's customer software support center at **1-800-437-3715** (8:30-4:00 ET) and give a detailed description of the problem.

Setting Up Student Data Files

Students' CP3 work can be stored on student data disks or on a local or network hard-disk drive.

Storing Student Work on CP3 Data Disks

The default location for storing student work is a CP3 data disk in floppy disk drive A. If you installed CP3 specifying either floppy disk drive A or B for storing student data, simply provide each student with a CP3 data disk and have students insert their data disk into the appropriate floppy disk drive when starting CP3.

■ **Tip:** Before using CP3, make a back-up copy of the data disks.

Storing Student Work in Data Directories

We recommend that students' data files be stored on CP3 data disks, which are included in the student packages. If want to store student data files on a local or network hard-disk drive, you will need approximately 2MB of disk space per student. You will also need to set up data directories for your students.

If you installed CP3 and specified that student data would be stored on a hard-disk drive, a single data directory is created for storing one student's CP3 work. If you want additional students to store their work in data directories, you need to set up a new data directory and CP3 program icon for each student, as follows:

1. From the Windows Program Manager, choose *Run* from the File menu.
2. In the Command Line blank:
   - Type **x:\setup** (where "x:\" represents the CD-ROM drive letter) if you are using the CD-ROM version of CP3.
   - Type **x:\cp3\setup** (where "x:\cp3\" represents the drive and directory where CP3 is installed) if you are using the floppy-disk version of CP3.

   Click **OK**.
3. A dialog box asks you to select your CP3 data location. Select **Store data on hard-disk drive** and click **OK** to continue.
4. Specify the drive where you want to create a data directory and click **OK**.
5. Type a path and name for the data directory (make sure that the directory does not already exist) and click **OK**.
6. A dialog box tells you that set-up is complete. Click **OK**. You are now back at the Program Manager.

The set-up program puts a new CP3 program icon (indicating the data directory location you specified) in the Glencoe Keyboarding program group. Each student must use a unique program icon (with a unique data directory location) when running CP3.

Setting Program Options

Cortez Peters' Championship Keyboarding Drills gives you control over a number of options so that you can customize the way students use the program. Before you or students use CP3 for the first time, you should access Program Options to view and/or change options according to your preferences. Each set of options is stored in a separate options file. You can set up more than one options file, but if you do so make sure that your students know which options file to select when they log on to CP3.

To access Program Options:

1. Start CP3 by double-clicking on the program icon in the Glencoe Keyboarding program group.
2. At the Log-on Information screen, choose *Instructor Options...* on the Help pull-down menu.
3. A dialog box asks for the password: key **teacher+** and click **OK**.

STOP ALERT: Keep the **teacher+** password confidential! It overrides the security provided by student passwords and gives access to options only the instructor should control.

4. In the Instructor Options dialog box (Figure 2-3), click **Program Options**.

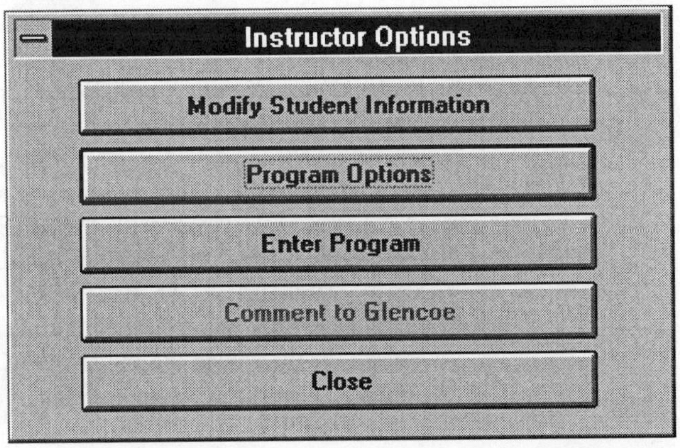

FIGURE 2-3: INSTRUCTOR OPTIONS DIALOG BOX

5. The Options File Editor dialog box (Figure 2-4) lists all of the existing options files. The first time you use the Options program, only a "STANDARD" file exists, containing these default settings: log-on password required, 5 Skill-Development Paragraph attempts per day, and either no Rhythm Development Drills included (floppy-disk version) or Rhythm Development Drills included with audio coming from the CD-ROM drive (CD-ROM version).

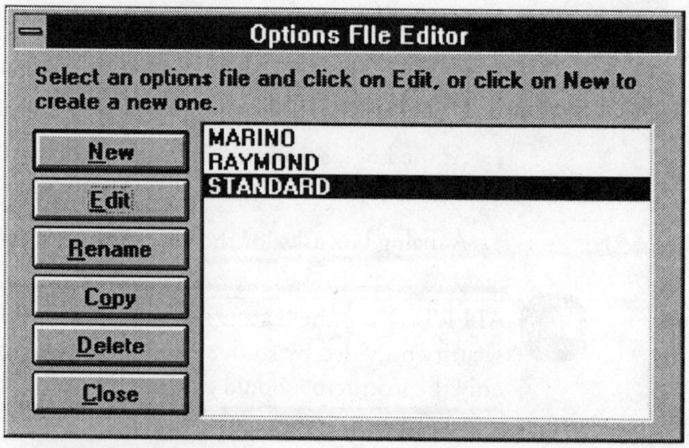

FIGURE 2-4: OPTIONS FILE EDITOR DIALOG BOX

To create a new options file:

a. Choose **New**.

b. In the Create Options File dialog box, type a name for the new file and click **OK**.

c. The Edit Options File dialog box displays settings (using defaults). Use the mouse to move to a setting you want to change and make the desired change. For information about the specific settings in an options file, see the Options File Settings table, below. To make a copy of an options file, highlight the file name on the list and click **Copy**. Then key a name for the copied file and click **OK**.

d. When all settings are what you want, click **Save** to save your new options file.

To view or change an existing options file:

a. Highlight the file name on the list and click **Edit**.

b. The Edit Options File dialog box displays the current settings for the options file. Use the mouse to move to a setting you want to change and make the desired change. For information about the specific settings in an options file, see the Options File Settings table, below.

c. When you are finished working with the settings, click **Save** to save your changes.

To call the options file by a different name:

a. Highlight the file name on the list and choose **Rename**.

b. In the Rename Options File dialog box, type a new name for the file and click **OK**.

To delete an options file:

a. Highlight its file name on the list and click **Delete**.
b. A message asks if you are sure that you want to delete the options file: click **Yes** to delete the file or **No** to return to the Options File Editor dialog box without deleting the selected file.

6. The program returns to the Options File Editor dialog box, where you can work on other options files if you wish. If you are finished working with options files, click **Close**.

❖ **Note:** Make sure that you tell your students which options file to use when they log on to CP3.

Options File Settings

Log-on Password Required	This setting should be checked (the default) if you want to require students to enter their password each time they log on to CP3. If this check box is not checked, the Password log-on field will be inactive.
Include Rhythm Development Drills	This setting should be checked (the default for the CD-ROM version) if you want Rhythm Development drills to be listed on and accessible from the Main Menu. If this check box is not checked (the default for the floppy-disk version), students will not be able to access any Rhythm Development drills. If you have installed the floppy-disk version of CP3 but you have the Rhythm Development audiocassettes (available separately from Glencoe), your students can listen to the audiocassettes while they enter drill lines in CP3. Click on the check box to change the setting. See "Rhythm Development Sentences drills," pages 49-51 for more information.
Use WAV Files for Audio	This setting should be checked if you installed the CD-ROM version of CP3 and you want the audio for Rhythm Development Sentences drills to be played from the CD-ROM. If you installed the CD-ROM version but would prefer to use the Rhythm Development audiocassettes for Rhythm Development Sentences drills, this setting should be unchecked. Click on the check box to change the setting.
Number of attempts on Skill-Development Paragraphs	If the Five radio button is selected (the default) for this setting, the student will have a maximum of 5 attempts at Skill-Development Paragraphs on a given day. The other option is 10 attempts per day. Click the radio button for the desired number of attempts per day.

Chapter 3: Start-Up and Operation

Starting the Program

1. If work is to be stored on student data disks, insert the data disk into the floppy drive.
2. Get into Windows and open the Glencoe Keyboarding program group.
3. Double-click on the appropriate program icon. (See "Setting Up Student Data Files" for more information about CP3 program icons.)
4. The opening sequence shows the title and copyright screens, followed by a photo or video clip of Cortez Peters and then the Log-on Information screen. The sequence advances automatically. However, you can advance to the next screen more quickly by clicking anywhere on the screen.

Initial Log-on The first time the student uses CP3, the Log-on Information screen (Figure 3-1) needs to be completed.

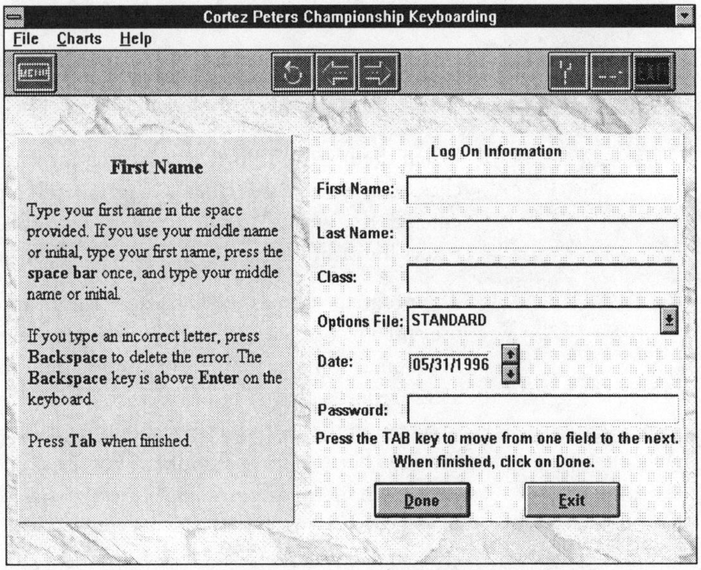

FIGURE 3-1: LOG-ON INFORMATION SCREEN

To complete the Log-on Information:

1. The student keys his or her first name, last name, and class name, using the **Tab** key or a mouse click to move from one field to the next. The student must complete the First Name and Last Name field. The Class field is optional.

2. In the Options File list box, the default STANDARD options file is selected. To use a different options file, the student clicks on the down arrow button to the right of the Options File list box and clicks on the name of the desired options file. For more information about options files, see "Setting Program Options," pages 10-13.

3. The computer's date appears in the Date field. If the computer's date is incorrect, the Date can be changed by clicking on the month, day, or year field and then using the up or down arrow button to adjust the number up or down.

4. If the options file setting for Log-on Password Required is off (unchecked), the Password field is inactive. Otherwise, the student keys a password of up to eight characters in the Password field. Note that asterisks (***) appear instead of what is keyed so that others cannot see the password. If the student forgets his or her password, you must assign a new one through *Instructor Options...* (from the Help pull-down menu) because the old one cannot be retrieved.

❖ **Note:** The text box in the left part of the Log-on Information screen tells the student how to complete the selected field.

5. When the Log-on Information screen is completed, the student clicks **Done** or presses **Enter** to continue. If a password was entered, the Verify Password dialog box displays: the student rekeys his or her password and clicks **OK** or presses **Enter**.

6. The program records the student's Log-on Information for future use and advances to the Introduction, which explains how to use the toolbar to navigate in CP3 and the pull-down menus to access reports, charts, and on-screen Help. To move from screen to screen in the Introduction, the student uses the Next and Previous buttons on the toolbar. For specific toolbar buttons and pull-down menu options, see "Toolbar" (page 41) and "Pull-Down Menus" (pages 38-40).

7. At the last Introduction screen, the student clicks the Next button to begin the Warmup exercise, which the student does at

the beginning of each CP3 session. See "Doing the Warmup," below, for more information.

❖ **Note:** The student goes through the Introduction at the time of initial log-on only. To access the Introduction subsequently, the student can select *Introduction* on the Help menu or press **Ctrl+I**.

Subsequent Log-ons

When the student returns to CP3 after initial log-on, the only information missing is the password, if it is required: the student keys his or her password and clicks **OK** or presses **Enter**. Note that the student can change the Date and Options File fields, but generally should not do so unless directed to by the instructor.

The program takes the student to the introduction/directions screen for the Warmup exercise. After the student finishes the Warmup exercise, the program goes to the Main Menu.

Doing the Warmup

After the student logs on to CP3, the first activity is the Warmup exercise. The Warmup is timed to last for 5 minutes and consists of a series of seven drill lines, each focusing on a different row or combination of rows on the keyboard. Word wrap is off for Warmup drills and editing is disabled. Warmup drills are saved but are not scored.

Here is how the Warmup exercise works:

1. The first Warmup screen provides directions and goals for the exercise. To begin keying the exercise, the student clicks the Next button on the toolbar. If the student prefers keying the drills from the textbook, he or she turns to the appropriate page in the textbook (indicated in the status bar at the bottom of the screen).
2. The Warmup input screen (Figure 3-2) displays with the first drill line at the top of the screen and the insertion point in a yellow window below the drill line. The student keys the drill line and presses **Enter**. The student can key the drill line from the displayed line on the screen or from the textbook. The appropriate text page is indicated in the status bar at the bottom of the screen.

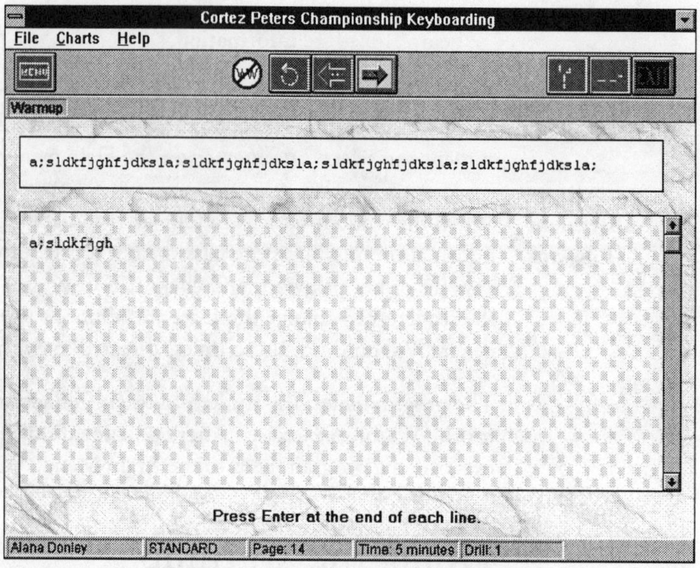

FIGURE 3-2: WARMUP INPUT SCREEN

3. The next drill line displays at the top of the input screen. The student continues typing drill lines, pressing **Enter** at the end of each line to begin the next line. The drill lines repeat if the student keys all seven lines before the 5 minute time is up.
4. At any time during the Warmup, the student can click the Next button to proceed to the Main Menu. If the student keys the Warmup for the full 5 minutes, a dialog box announces when time is up: the student clicks **OK** to proceed to the Main Menu.

Main Menu

When the student logs on to CP3, the first activity is a 5-minute Warmup. At any time during the Warmup exercise, the student may advance to the Main Menu (Figure 3-3) by clicking the Next button on the toolbar. If the student uses the full 5 minutes allotted for the Warmup, the program announces when time is up: the student clicks **OK** to advance to the Main Menu.

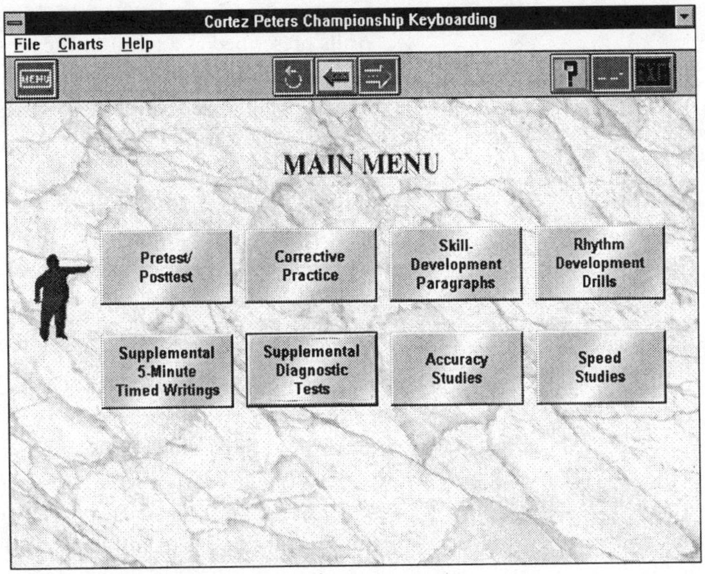

FIGURE 3-3: MAIN MENU

The Main Menu consists of two rows of buttons. The top row presents the recommended activities in a planned cycle arrangement that Cortez Peters recommends in the textbook. The bottom row presents activities by group rather than in a planned cycle. The activities can be selected and done in any sequence by themselves or in combination with the cycle activities (as supplemental exercises).

The Main Menu includes these items:

Displays the Pretest/Posttest Menu, which lists 10 Pretests and 10 Posttests. Pretests, which consist of a 5-Minute Timed Writing and a Diagnostic Test, are designed to be taken at the beginning of a cycle. They are used to diagnose keyboarding problems and prescribe practice to correct those problems. Posttests, which are exactly the same as the corresponding Pretests, are to be taken after the student completes the corrective practice (prescribed from the Pretest), to measure improvements in speed and accuracy. For detailed information on how the Pretest/Posttest exercises work, see "5-Minute Timed Writings" and "Diagnostic Tests" in Chapter 4.

Displays the Corrective Practice Menu, which lists the drills prescribed as a result of the most recent Pretest 5-Minute Timed Writing and/or Diagnostic Test. Corrective Practice consists of a series of exercises in prioritized order (high to low). Accuracy Studies from Chart 2 (5-Minute Timed Writings) are listed first followed by Accuracy Studies from Chart 3 (Diagnostic Tests), Speed Studies from Chart 3, and, finally, Misspelled Words. See "Accuracy Studies," "Speed Studies," and "Misspelled Words" in Chapter 4 for details on the Corrective Practice exercises.

❖ **Note:** The Corrective Practice Menu always includes Misspelled Words which, when selected, accesses a blank practice screen where word wrap is off, editing is disabled, and activities are untimed and unscored. This blank practice screen is accessible only from the Corrective Practice Menu and can be used for any type of keying practice—including, but not limited to, misspelled words.

Starts the Skill-Development Paragraphs exercise, which is intended to be done during the last five or ten minutes of each corrective practice hour. CP3 takes the student to the first Skill-Development Paragraph the student has not completed error-free. The student cannot select a level for Skill-Development Paragraphs, but you can change the program-determined level by using Instructor Options to modify the student's information (see "Correcting Log-on Information," pages 36-38). For more information, see "Skill-Development Paragraphs" in Chapter 4.

Displays the Rhythm Development Drill Menu, which displays a list of 8 tape/drill exercises. A Rhythm Development tape/drill is equivalent to one side from the Cortez Peters Rhythm Development Tapes and includes a Sentences drill and a Skillbuilding drill. The Rhythm Development item does not appear on the Main Menu if the Include Rhythm Development Drills setting is off (unchecked) in the selected options file (see "Setting Program Options" in Chapter 2 for more information on options files). For more information, see "Rhythm Development Sentences" and "Rhythm Development Skillbuilding" in Chapter 4.

Displays the Supplemental Timed Writings Menu, which is used to take a 5-Minute Timed Writing that is not part of a Pretest/Posttest. These timed writings can be used if the student is not following the recommended cycle approach or as supplemental activities to the cycle approach. For more information about this type of exercise, see "5-Minute Timed Writings" in Chapter 4.

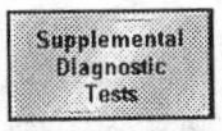

Displays the Supplemental Diagnostic Tests Menu, which is used to take a Diagnostic Test that is not part of a Pretest/Posttest. These Diagnostic Tests can be used if the student is not following the recommended cycle approach or as supplemental activities to the cycle approach. For more information about this type of exercise, see "Diagnostic Tests" in Chapter 4.

Displays the Accuracy Study Menu, which is used to access all Accuracy Study drills (including those listed on the Corrective Practice Menu). For more information, see "Accuracy Studies" in Chapter 4.

Displays the Speed Study Menu, which is used to access all Speed Study drills (including those listed on the Corrective Practice Menu). For more information, see "Speed Studies" in Chapter 4.

❖ **Note:** A red check mark preceding an exercise on a menu indicates that the exercise has been completed. A hollow check mark indicates that the exercise has been started but not completed. Only the Skill-Development Paragraph Menu has no list of exercises since the student is not given the option of selecting the paragraph to be keyed.

Working on Exercises

To work on an exercise, the student:

1. Logs on and does the Warmup.

❖ **Note:** To access a blank screen for additional practice, click on the Corrective Practice button from the Main Menu and select Misspelled words. In this practice screen, word wrap is off, editing is disabled, and activities are untimed and unscored.

2. Selects an item on the Main Menu and a specific activity or exercise on the selected menu.

3. Reads the introduction/directions screen (Figure 3-4) to find out the goal, duration, word wrap setting, charting, and how-to instructions for completing the exercise.

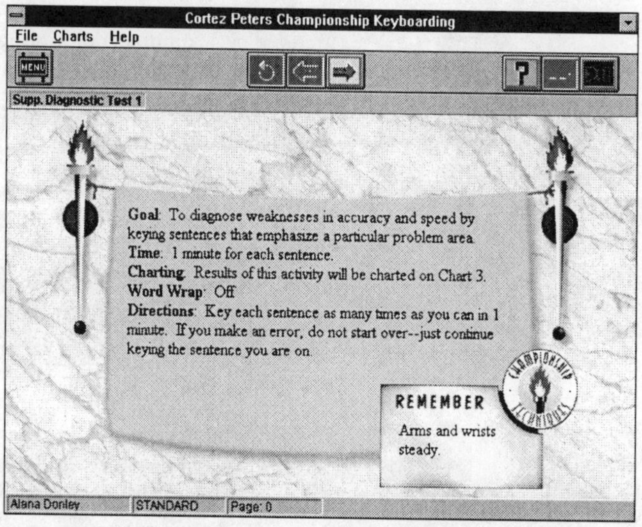

FIGURE 3-4: EXERCISE INTRODUCTION/DIRECTIONS SCREEN

4. Turns to the appropriate page in the textbook and clicks the Next button on the toolbar or presses **F6** to continue.

5. Keys the text for the exercise in the input screen (Figure 3-5).

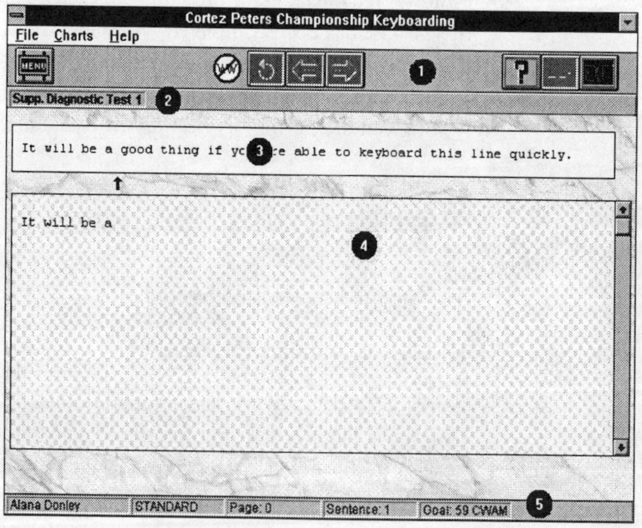

FIGURE 3-5: EXERCISE INPUT SCREEN

Note the following parts of the exercise input screen:

❶ Toolbar: lists icons for navigation and on-screen guidance and word wrap status.

❷ Dialog bar: specifies the exercise name and the student's scores on exercise work completed.

❸ Drill line: This is the copy the student keys. In 5-Minute Timed Writings and Skill-Development Paragraphs, there is no drill line; the student must key from the textbook.

❹ Input area: The student keys the copy for the exercise in this scrolling window.

❺ Status bar: specifies the student name, options file being used, textbook page and drill line numbers, and goals (where applicable).

❖ **Note:** All exercise screens have the same basic layout, although each type of exercise works somewhat differently. For information about specific types of exercises and how they work, see Chapter 4.

6. Reviews his or her scored text (for scored exercises).

At any point, the student can exit the program by selecting *Exit* on the File menu or exit the exercise by clicking the Menu button or pressing **Esc**. If the student exits the program while in an exercise, in most cases that exercise will be considered incomplete and the student will be able to resume work on the exercise when returning to CP3 at a later time.

Using the Corrective Practice Menu

If you are using the structured, cycle approach to CP3, your students will start each cycle by taking a Pretest, which consists of a 5-Minute Timed Writing and a Diagnostic Test. Based on the results of these activities, CP3 diagnoses problems and weaknesses and prescribes practice drills to remedy those problems and weaknesses. The prescriptions resulting from the most recent Pretest (5-Minute Timed Writing and/or Diagnostic Test) are listed on the Corrective Practice Menu, which is accessible from the Main Menu. Because Posttests are taken for comparative purposes only, corrective practice drills are not prescribed from Posttest activities.

The Corrective Practice Menu is a *dynamic* menu because the drills can be accessed directly from the menu and each activity's completion is automatically indicated by a checkmark. Although a list of prescribed drills can be viewed and/or printed at any time for any Pretest activity from the Charts pull-down menu, the *dynamic* Corrective Practice Menu will be available only for the most recent Pretest activity (5-Minute Timed Writing *or* Diagnostic Test) or activities (5-Minute Timed Writing *and* Diagnostic Test). When the 5-Minute Timed Writing and Diagnostic Test from the same Pretest are taken in sequence (as is recommended), the resulting Corrective Practice Menu contains the combined drills from both activities in prioritized order.

A 5-Minute Timed Writing or Diagnostic Test taken from another Pretest will generate a new Corrective Practice Menu which will erase the assignments of the previous Pretest. Make your students aware of this feature, and caution them to not take any activity from another Pretest until the current dynamic Corrective Practice Menu is no longer needed.

Students should use the Corrective Practice Menu to guide their practice sessions in the cycle approach, as follows:

1. After completing the Pretest (both the 5-Minute Timed Writing and the Diagnostic Test), the student accesses the Corrective Practice Menu by clicking the Corrective Practice button on the Main Menu, selects the first drill on the Corrective Practice Menu, and completes the drill.

2. At the completion of the drill, the program returns to the Corrective Practice Menu and marks the drill complete.

3. The student selects the next drill on the Corrective Practice Menu and completes that drill. The student continues working on drills listed on the Corrective Practice Menu until all drills are completed or until the student takes a Posttest. If the student takes a 5-Minute Timed Writing or Diagnostic Test from another Pretest, a new Corrective Practice Menu will be generated and assignments from the last Corrective Practice Menu will be erased.

4. After the student completes the 5-Minute Timed Writing or Diagnostic Test for the next Pretest, the Corrective Practice Menu is recreated and all completion marks for Speed Study and Accuracy Study drills are erased.

5. The student uses the new Corrective Practice Menu to work on drills prescribed as a result of the new Pretest.

❖ **Note:** The Corrective Practice Menu is generated only from Pretest activities. Supplemental 5-Minute Timed Writings and Supplemental Diagnostic Tests generate a list of prescribed corrective practice activities (accessible from Charts 2 and 3), but these are not available from the Corrective Practice Menu.

Playing Videos (CD-ROM Version Only)

The opening sequence and the program Introduction include video clips, which play automatically if the student is running the CD-ROM version of CP3. To bypass the opening video, press **Esc**.

Additional videos are available on the Video Menu (Figure 3-6) in the CD-ROM version.

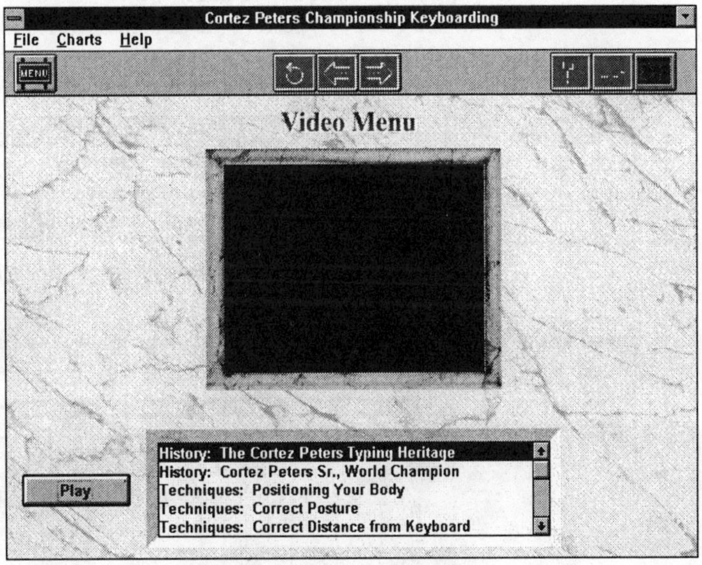

FIGURE 3-6: VIDEO MENU

To play a video clip on the Video Menu:

1. The student accesses the Video Menu by clicking the Video button on the toolbar, selecting *Video...* on the File pull-down menu, or pressing **Ctrl+V**.

❖ **Note:** In order to access the Video Menu, the student must be at a menu. The Video Menu is not accessible from within an exercise.

2. The student uses the scroll bar to move through the list of video clips, selects (highlights) the desired video clip, and clicks Play.
3. The video clip plays. At any time, the student can stop the video clip by clicking anywhere on the screen.
4. When the clip finishes playing, the program returns to the Video Menu. From there, the student can play other video clips or click the Menu button on the toolbar to return to the previous menu.

❖ **Note:** If the video clips appear very dark on the computer monitor, turn up the monitor's brightness level.

Viewing and Printing Charts

All charting is done automatically by CP3. The student can view or print any chart by selecting the desired chart from the Charts pull-down menu (Figure 3-7).

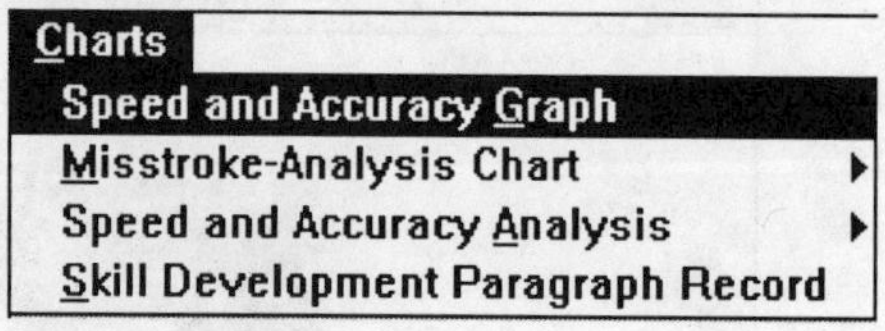

FIGURE 3-7: CHARTS PULL-DOWN MENU

Speed and Accuracy Graph (Chart 1)

The Speed and Accuracy Chart (Figure 3-8) is a bar graph that plots all of the student's 5-Minute Timed Writings.

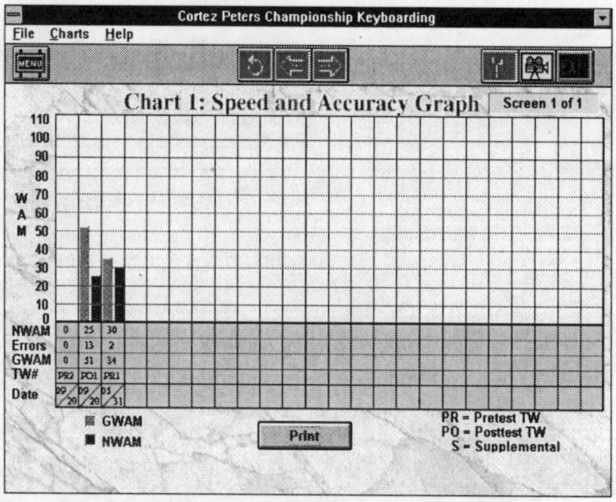

FIGURE 3-8: SPEED AND ACCURACY

For each timed writing, the student's GWAM (gross words a minute) is plotted in green and NWAM (net words a minute) in red. NWAM is equal to GWAM minus 2 times the number of errors. Below the bars for each timed writing are the student's scores, the exercise identifier ("PR" represents a Pretest timed writing, "PO" represents a Posttest timed writing, and "S" represents a Supplemental 5-Minute Timed Writing), and the date the timed writing was taken.

To print a copy of the chart, the student clicks the **Print** button at the bottom of the screen.

If the student has completed more than 24 5-Minute Timed Writings, the chart extends to multiple screens, in which case the student clicks the Next and Previous buttons on the toolbar to move among the chart screens. To exit the chart, the student clicks the Menu button on the toolbar.

❖ **Note:** When two attempts have been made for a 5-Minute Timed Writing, only the better attempt is charted.

Misstroke-Analysis Chart (Chart 2)

When the student selects *Misstroke-Analysis Chart* on the Charts pull-down menu, a submenu displays three options: Pretest/Posttest Timed Writing, Supplemental Timed Writing, and Summary of Timed Writings.

Pretest/Posttest Timed Writing

If the student selects this option, Chart 2: Misstroke Analysis (Figure 3-9) shows an analysis of the most recently completed Pretest or Posttest 5-Minute Timed Writing (whichever was completed most recently). The analysis shows errors by hand, finger, and letter and classifies each error by type (punctuation, shifting, spacing, and concentration).

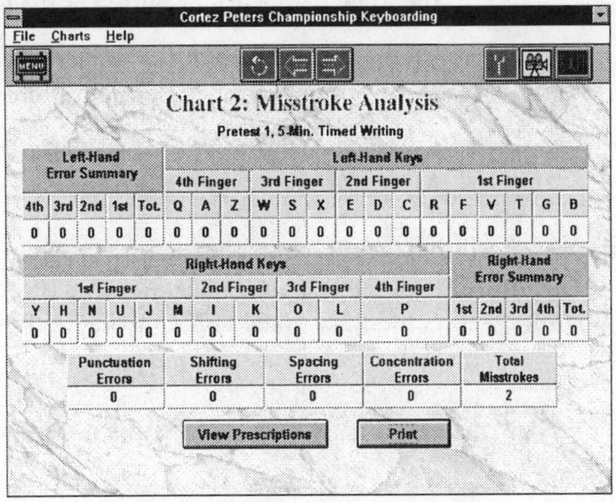

FIGURE 3-9: MISSTROKE ANALYSIS

To print a copy of the chart, the student clicks the **Print** button at the bottom of the chart screen.

To view a list of prescribed corrective practice for a Pretest 5-Minute Timed Writing, the student clicks the **View Prescriptions** button at the bottom of the chart screen (this button does not appear for Posttest 5-Minute Timed Writings). The prescriptions screen lists the corrective practice exercises, which the user can print by clicking the **Print** button. To return to the chart from the prescriptions list, the student clicks the **View Chart** button.

❖ **Note:** The prescriptions that appear with Chart 2 for Pretest 5-Minute Timed Writings also appear on the Corrective Practice Menu. Each time the student takes a new Pretest, the Corrective Practice Menu changes to reflect the prescriptions from the new Pretest.

To exit the Misstroke Analysis Chart, the student clicks the Menu button on the toolbar.

Supplemental Timed Writing If the student selects this option, Chart 2: Misstroke Analysis shows the misstroke analysis for the most recently completed Supplemental 5-Minute Timed Writing. The list of corrective practice exercises prescribed based on the error analysis is also available. The chart and prescriptions list look exactly like those for a Pretest 5-Minute Timed Writing (see Figure 3-9):

- To print a copy of the chart or prescriptions, the student clicks the **Print** button at the bottom of the chart or prescriptions screen.
- To see the list of prescribed corrective practice, the student clicks the **View Prescriptions** button at the bottom of the chart screen.
- To see the chart again, the student clicks the **View Chart** button at the bottom of the prescriptions screen.
- To exit the Misstroke Analysis Chart, the student clicks the Menu button on the toolbar.

Summary of Timed Writings If the student selects this option, the Misstroke Analysis: Summary Chart for 5-Minute Timed Writings (Figure 3-10) lists a one-line entry for every timed writing (whether Pretest, Posttest, or Supplemental) the student has completed. This Summary Chart gives the student access to the Misstroke Analysis chart for any completed 5-Minute Timed Writing (not just the most recent one).

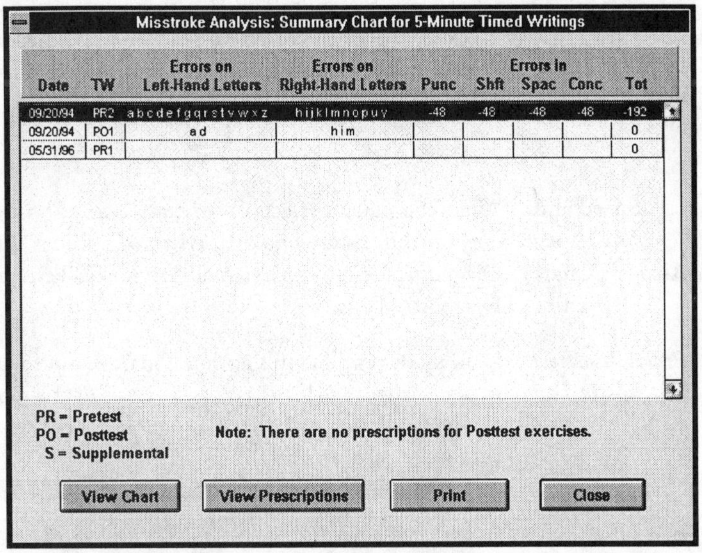

FIGURE 3-10: MISSTROKE ANALYSIS: SUMMARY CHART FOR TIMED WRITING

Each entry on the summary chart includes the following items:

- Date 5-Minute Timed Writing was taken.
- Timed writing identifier. "PR" represents a Pretest timed writing, "PO" represents a Posttest timed writing, and "S" represents a Supplemental 5-Minute Timed Writing.
- Errors on Left-Hand Letters. List of all left-hand keys that had errors.
- Errors on Right-Hand Letters. List of all right-hand keys that had errors.
- Errors in punctuation, shifting, spacing, and concentration, as well as total errors.

To work with the summary chart, the student:

- Clicks the **Print** button at the bottom of the chart or prescriptions screen to print a copy of the chart or prescriptions list.
- Selects a 5-Minute Timed Writing and clicks **View Chart** to see the complete Chart 2: Misstroke Analysis for the selected timed writing.

- Selects a 5-Minute Timed Writing and clicks **View Prescriptions** to see the list of corrective practice prescribed on the basis of a Pretest or Supplemental 5-Minute Timed Writing.
- Clicks the Menu button on the toolbar to exit the summary chart.

Speed and Accuracy Analysis Chart (Chart 3)

When the student selects *Speed and Accuracy* on the Charts pull-down menu, a submenu displays three options: Pretest/Posttest Diagnostic Test, Supplemental Diagnostic Test, and Summary of Diagnostic Tests.

Pretest/Posttest Diagnostic Test

If the student selects this option, Chart 3: Speed and Accuracy Analysis (Figure 3-11) shows an analysis of the most recently completed Pretest or Posttest Diagnostic Test (whichever was completed most recently).

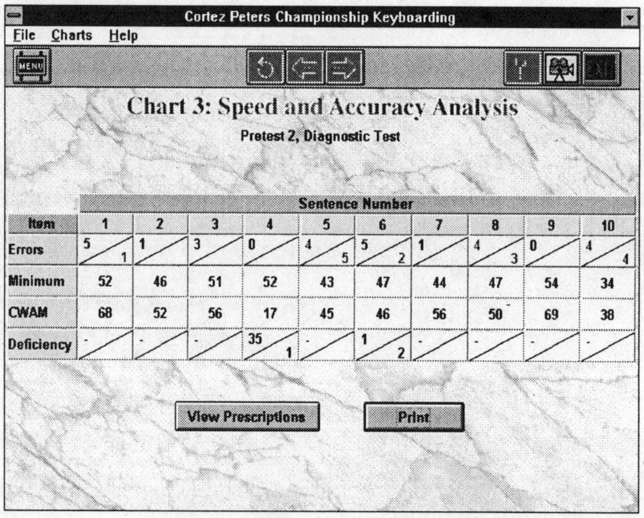

	Sentence Number									
Item	1	2	3	4	5	6	7	8	9	10
Errors	5 / 1	1 /	3 /	0 /	4 / 5	5 / 2	1 /	4 / 3	0 /	4 / 4
Minimum	52	46	51	52	43	47	44	47	54	34
CWAM	68	52	56	17	45	46	56	50	69	38
Deficiency	- /	- /	- /	35 / 1	- /	1 / 2	- /	- /	- /	- /

FIGURE 3-11: SPEED AND ACCURACY ANALYSIS

For each sentence of the Diagnostic Test, the analysis shows:

- Errors. In the upper left corner of the box, the number of errors the student made on the sentence (appears in red if greater than 3). In the lower right corner of the box, the order in the prioritized sequence in which the corrective practice should be done for the sentence (if the student made more than 3 errors).
- Minimum. The minimum CWAM (correct words a minute) speed the student is supposed to achieve for the sentence.
- CWAM. The student's CWAM on the sentence. CWAM is calculated as gross words a minute minus one times the number of errors.

- Deficiency: In the upper left corner, the magnitude of the student's speed shortfall (Minimum minus CWAM). In the lower right corner, the order in the prioritized sequence in which the corrective practice should be done for the sentence (if the upper left corner of the box reflects a deficiency).

To print a copy of the chart, the student clicks the **Print** button at the bottom of the chart screen.

To view a list of prescribed corrective practice for a Pretest Diagnostic Test, the student clicks the **View Prescriptions** button at the bottom of the chart screen (this button does not appear for Posttest Diagnostic Tests). The prescriptions screen lists the corrective practice exercises, which the user can print by clicking the **Print** button. To return to the chart, the student clicks the **View Chart** button.

To exit the Speed and Accuracy Analysis, the student clicks the Menu button on the toolbar.

Supplemental Diagnostic Test

If the student selects this option, Chart 3: Speed and Accuracy Analysis shows the analysis for the most recently completed Supplemental Diagnostic Test. The list of corrective practice exercises prescribed based on the analysis is also available. The chart and prescriptions list look exactly like those for a Pretest Diagnostic Test (see Figure 3-11):

- To print a copy of the chart or prescriptions list, the student clicks the **Print** button at the bottom of the chart or prescriptions screen.
- To see the list of prescribed corrective practice, the student clicks the **View Prescriptions** button at the bottom of the chart screen.
- To see the chart again, the student clicks the **View Chart** button at the bottom of the prescriptions screen.
- To exit the Speed and Accuracy Analysis, the student clicks the Menu button on the toolbar.

Summary of Diagnostic Tests

If the student selects this option, the Speed and Accuracy Analysis: Summary Chart for Diagnostic Tests (Figure 3-12) lists a one-line entry for every Diagnostic Test (whether Pretest, Posttest, or Supplemental) the student has completed. This Summary Chart gives the student access to the Speed and Accuracy Analysis chart for any completed Diagnostic Test (not just the most recent one).

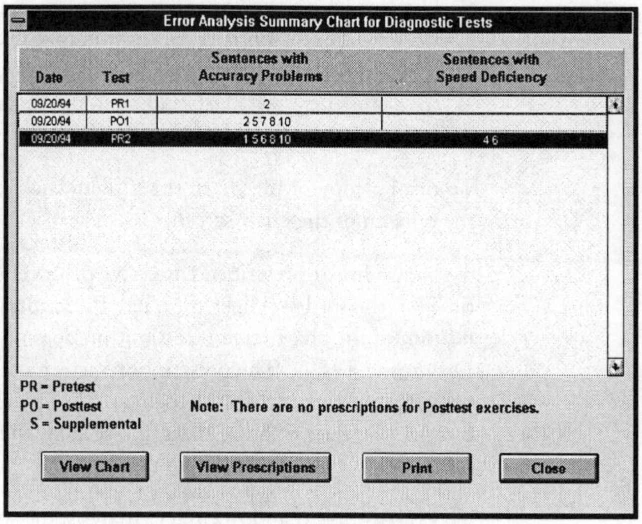

FIGURE 3-12: SPEED AND ACCURACY ANALYSIS: SUMMARY CHART FOR DIAGNOSTIC TESTS

Each entry on the summary chart includes the following items:

- Date Diagnostic Test was taken.
- Diagnostic Test identifier. "PR" represents a Pretest Diagnostic Test, "PO" represents a Posttest Diagnostic Test, and "S" represents a Supplemental Diagnostic Test.
- Sentences with Accuracy Problems. List of the numbers of all sentences in which the student made more than 3 errors.
- Sentences with Speed Deficiency. List of the numbers of all sentences in which the student's CWAM was less than the Minimum.

To work with the summary chart, the student:

- Clicks the **Print** button at the bottom of the screen to print the summary chart.
- Selects a Diagnostic Test and clicks **View Chart** to see the complete Chart 3: Speed and Accuracy Analysis for the selected Diagnostic Test.
- Selects a Diagnostic Test and clicks **View Prescriptions** to see the list of corrective practice prescribed on the basis of a Pretest or Supplemental Diagnostic Test.

- Clicks the Menu button on the toolbar to exit the summary chart.

Skill-Development Paragraph Record (Chart 4)

The Skill-Development Paragraph Record (Figure 3-13) is a chart that records the date each paragraph was keyed in one minute without an error.

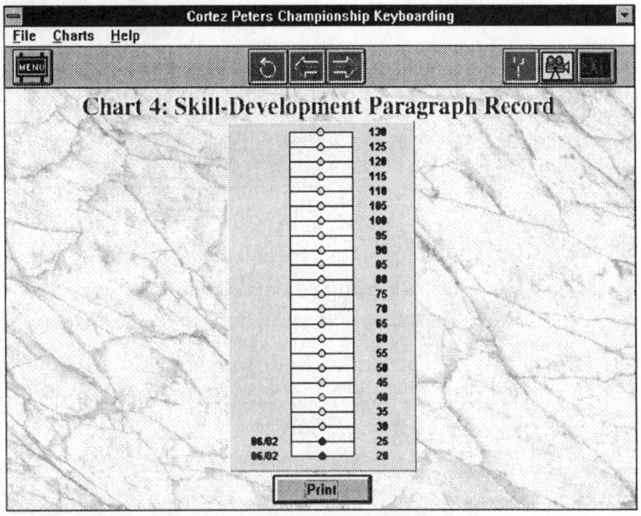

FIGURE 3-13: CHART 4: SKILL-DEVELOPMENT PARAGRAPH RECORD

To print a copy of the graph, the student clicks the **Print** button at the bottom of the screen.

Viewing and Printing Reports

CP3 keeps two types of reports for each student. The Summary Report provides a snapshot of all exercises the student has worked on, with results and completion status for each. Detailed Reports include the scored text for any exercise the student has worked on—unless the student has used the *Delete Files...* option on the File pull-down menu to delete the text for one or more types of exercises (see "Deleting Work Files," pages 35-36).

To access the student's reports:

1. The student selects the *Report...* option on the File pull-down menu. The Report Options dialog box (Figure 3-14) displays.

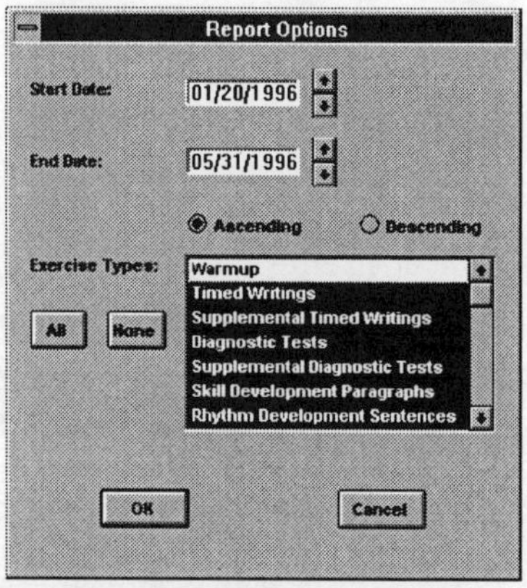

FIGURE 3-14: REPORT OPTIONS DIALOG BOX

2. The student specifies a date range, sort order (ascending or descending by date), and exercise type(s) to include in the Summary Report, and then clicks **OK** or presses **Enter**.

3. The Summary Report window (figure 3-15) lists all of the exercises that the student specified for Report Options, one exercise per line.

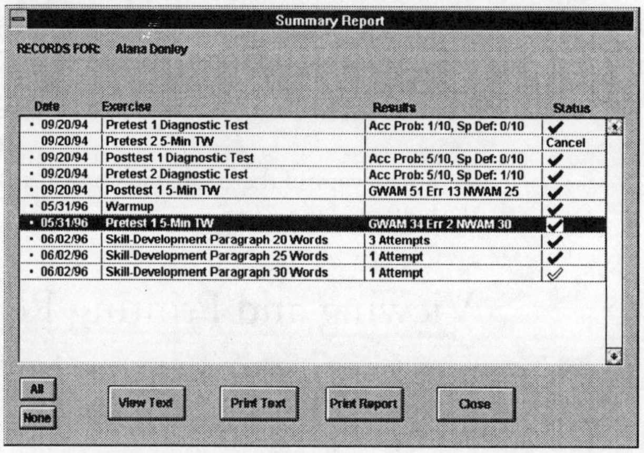

FIGURE 3-15: SUMMARY REPORT WINDOW

Each line on the Summary Report includes the date the student last worked on the exercise, the exercise name, the scoring results (generally blank unless the exercise has been completed), and the completion status (a red check mark designates complete, a hollow check mark designates partially complete).

4. To print a copy of the Summary Report, the student clicks **Print Report**. To print a copy of the scored text for any exercises, the student clicks once on the lines for the desired exercises (they must be preceded by a black bullet) and then clicks **Print Text**.

5. To view the text for any exercises (that is, get a Detailed Report), the student clicks on the desired exercise lines on the Summary Report (they must be preceded by a black bullet) and clicks **View Text**. The Detailed Report window (Figure 3-16) displays the student's text and scores.

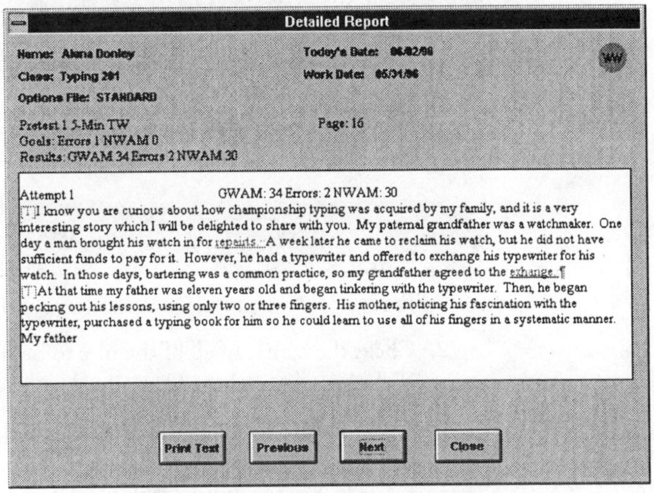

FIGURE 3-16: DETAILED REPORT WINDOW

- To print the Detailed Report, the student clicks **Print Text**.
- If the student selected more than one exercise to view text for, the student uses the **Next** and **Previous** buttons to move among the Detailed Reports.
- When finished viewing the Detailed Reports, the student clicks **Close** to return to the Summary Report.

6. To exit the Summary Report, the student clicks **Close**.

Deleting Work Files

CP3 stores the student's work on a student data disk or in a student directory on a hard disk. For each type of exercise, the student's work is stored in a different file. At any time, the student can delete the text for all exercises of a particular type.

❖ **Note:** When *Delete Files...* is used, just the student's text (Detailed Report) is deleted. Scores for deleted text files will be retained on the Summary Report, and data for charts and prescriptions will also be retained.

To delete work for particular types of exercises, the student:

1. Selects *Delete Files...* on the File pull-down menu. The Delete Detailed Report Files dialog box (Figure 3-17) indicates the names and sizes of the files that can be deleted, one file per exercise type.

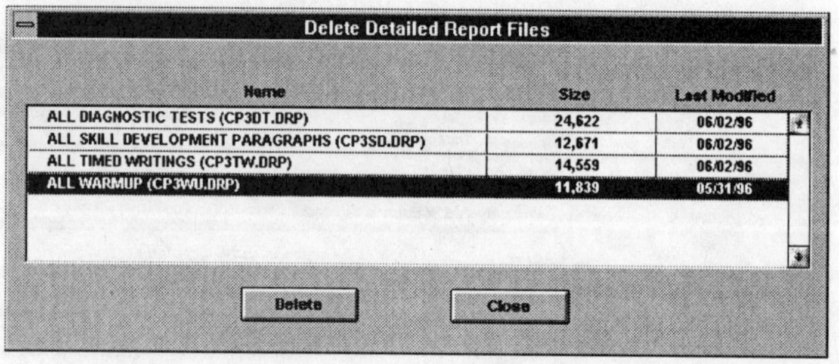

FIGURE 3-17: DELETE DETAILED REPORT FILES WINDOW

2. Clicks the names of all of the files to be deleted. (The student clicks on a highlighted file to deselect it.)

3. Clicks **Delete** to delete the selected file(s). The Confirm dialog box displays. The student:
   - Clicks **Yes** to confirm each file deletion individually.
   - Clicks **Yes to All** to confirm all file deletions at one time.
   - Clicks **No** to save the selected file from being deleted.
   - Clicks **Cancel** to save all selected files and return to the Delete Detailed Report Files dialog box. To exit this function, the student clicks **Cancel** again.

Using Instructor Options

CP3's Instructor Options allow you to:

- Access a student's log-on information to make corrections, if necessary. See "Correcting Log-on Information," in this section.

- View and/or print a student's work without having to enter the student's password. See "Looking at a Student's Exercises," in this section.

- Create, modify, and delete options files, which control certain settings for running CP3. See "Setting Program Options," pages 10-13.

Correcting Log-on Information

When students initially log on to the program, their name, class, and password are recorded. From then on, students cannot change this information on their own. As the instructor, however, you have access to all Log-on Information and can make log-on corrections and changes for your students. You can also change the current Skill-Development Paragraph level for a student.

Here is how to change a student's Log-on Information or Skill-Development Paragraph level:

1. Start up the program using the student's data disk or data directory.
2. When the Log-on Information screen appears, select *Instructor Options...* on the Help pull-down menu.
3. A dialog box asks for the password: key **teacher+** and click **OK**.

❖ **Note:** Keep the **teacher+** password confidential! It overrides the security provided by student passwords and gives access to options only the instructor should control.

4. In the Instructor Options dialog box, click **Modify Student Information.**
5. The Modify Student Information dialog box (Figure 3-18) gives you access to all of the student's Log-on Information. Key the correct information, using the mouse or **Tab** key to move from field to field.
   - In the First Name field, type the student's first name and middle initial, if desired.
   - In the Last Name field, type the student's last name.
   - In the Class field, type the name of the student's class.
   - In the Password field, the student's password appears as a series of asterisks. You cannot view the original password. Rather, type a new password for the student, making sure to use a password that the student will remember but that other students are not likely to guess.
   - In the Skill-Development Paragraph level field, the student's current level (WAM speed) appears. Click the up or down arrow button to adjust the student's paragraph level up or down.

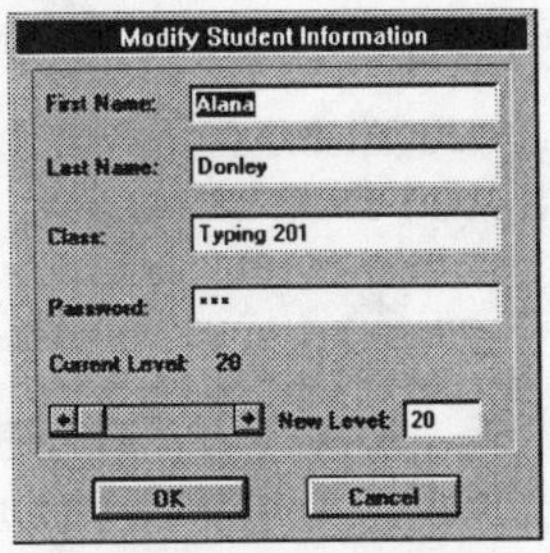

FIGURE 3-18: MODIFY STUDENT INFORMATION DIALOG BOX

6. When all information is correct, click OK.

Looking at a Student's Exercises

To look at a student's work without having to know the student's password:

1. Start up the program using the student's data disk or data directory.
2. When the Log-on Information screen appears, select *Instructor Options...* on the Help pull-down menu.
3. A dialog box asks for the password: key **teacher+** and click OK.

❖ **Note:** Keep the **teacher+** password confidential! It overrides the security provided by student passwords and gives access to options only the instructor should control.

4. In the Instructor Options dialog box, click **Enter Program**. The program takes you to the introduction/directions screen for the Warmup exercise. To advance to the Main Menu, where you can view the student's reports or charts, click the Next button twice (without keying the Warmup drills).

Navigation

CP3 uses the standard Windows interface conventions to make the software easy to use for anyone familiar with Windows.

❖ **Note:** If you are not familiar with Windows or using a mouse, it would be worthwhile for you to run the Windows tutorial, which comes with Windows 3.1 and is generally installed as part of the Windows 3.1 installation. Refer to your Windows 3.1 User's Guide for more information.

The toolbar and shortcut commands (see "Keyboard Shortcuts," pages 41-42) are used to navigate in CP3. The pull-down menus are for accessing reports, charts, and Help topics, deleting work files, and using CP3 Instructor Options.

Help is available at any point by pressing **F1** or choosing *Help* on the Help pull-down menu.

Pull-Down Menus

Pull-down menus can be accessed using a mouse or the keyboard.

- Mouse: click on a menu bar item to display its pull-down menu, and then double-click on the desired option.

- Keyboard: press the **Alt** key to activate the menu bar, key the highlighted letter of the desired menu, use the down arrow key to move to the desired option, and then press **Enter**.

To deactivate the menu bar, press **Alt** or click anywhere on the screen other than on the menu bar or in a pull-down menu.

File Menu

Report...

Report... is used to view or print a record of the student's work in CP3. The Summary Report lists exercise dates and results. From there, the student can access a Detailed Report for an exercise, which includes the student's full text and detailed scoring information for the exercise. For detailed information on this function, see "Viewing and Printing Reports," pages 33-35.

Delete Files...

Delete Files... is used to delete the student's text for specified types of exercises. When work (Detailed Report) files are deleted, just the student's scored text is deleted. Exercise results are preserved in the student's Summary Report and in charts and prescriptions. See "Deleting Work Files," pages 35-36.

Video... (Ctrl+V)

Video... is used to access the Video Menu, which lists a variety of video clips of Cortez Peters showing championship keyboarding techniques and recounting his championship typing heritage. For more information on CP3 videos, see "Playing Videos," pages 25-26.

Exit (Ctrl+X)

When the student selects *Exit*, a dialog box will ask if the student really wants to exit the program: clicking **OK** (the default) exits the program; clicking **Cancel** returns to CP3.

Charts Menu

Speed and Accuracy Graph

When the student selects *Speed and Accuracy Chart* on the Charts menu, Chart 1 identifies all of the student's 5-Minute Timed Writings, showing the date of the exercise and the student's GWAM, NWAM, and number of errors. For more information, see "Speed and Error Graph (Chart 1)" pages 26-27.

Misstroke Analysis

When the student selects *Misstroke Analysis* on the Charts menu, a pop-up menu displays these options: Pretest/Posttest Timed

Writing, Supplemental Timed Writing, and Summary of Timed Writings. See "Misstroke Analysis (Chart 2)," pages 27-28.

Speed and Accuracy Analysis

When the student selects *Speed and Accuracy Analysis* on the Charts menu, a pop-up menu displays these options: Pretest/Posttest Diagnostic Test, Supplemental Diagnostic Test, and Summary of Diagnostic Tests. For information about these charts, see "Speed and Accuracy Analysis (Chart 3)," pages 30-31.

Skill-Development Paragraph Record

When the student selects *Skill-Development Paragraph Record* on the Charts menu, CP3 displays a chart showing the dates the student successfully keyed a Skill-Development Paragraph in one minute without an error. For more information about this chart, see "Skill-Development Paragraph Record," page 33.

Help Menu

Help (F1)

Pressing **F1** or selecting *Help* on the Help menu displays the Help window with information about the current screen or activity.

Help Topics...

The *Help Topics...* option links to the Contents topic of the CP3 Help system, which lists the major topics covered in Help.

Introduction (Ctrl+I)

When the student selects *Introduction* from the Help menu or presses **Ctrl+I**, CP3 goes to the Introduction (which the student went through after logging on to CP3 for the first time). The student uses the Next and Previous buttons to navigate in the Introduction. At the last Introduction screen, clicking Next exits the Introduction.

Instructor Options...

Use *Instructor Options...* to work on options files, modify a student's Log-on Information, look at a student's work without having to enter a student password, or submit comments on CP3 to Glencoe. *Instructor Options...* are designed for your use only, not for use by students. See "Using Instructor Options," pages 36-38 for more information.

About...

The *About...* option will display program information, including the program name, version, date, etc.

Toolbar

The toolbar, which appears on all screens except for menus, consists of a row of buttons below the menu bar. When a button is inactive, it is gray on the toolbar. Use the buttons on the toolbar to move around within CP3. When you point to a button on the toolbar, a tooltip shows the name of the button and the keyboard shortcut, if there is one.

Menu (or **Esc**) takes the student to the previous menu.

Next (**F6**) takes the student to the next screen within an activity.

Previous (**Shft+F6**) takes the student to the previous screen within an activity (except when in the Main Menu).

Restart Timing (**Ctrl+R**) is active during the first 30 seconds of each attempt on a 5-Minute Timed Writing and for the duration of the Skill-Development Paragraph exercise. **Restart** allows the student to start the current timing or paragraph over, which is very helpful if the student realizes he or she has made a mistake such as typing the wrong text from the textbook or forgetting to tab or capitalize the first word.

Videos (**Ctrl+V**) takes the student to the Video Menu (CD-ROM version only).

Help (**F1**) takes the user to context-sensitive Help.

Exit (**Ctrl+X**) takes the student out of the program. The Exit button on the toolbar functions exactly the same as the *Exit* option on the File pull-down menu.

Keyboard Shortcuts

Sometimes it is easier to use a keyboard shortcut rather than to remove your hand from the keyboard to activate the mouse. Here are the keyboard shortcuts in CP3:

Alt	**Menu bar** Activates the menu bar.
Ctrl+R	**Restart timing** Allows the student to restart a Skill-Development Paragraph (at any time) or a 5-Minute Timed Writing (within the first 30 seconds only).
Ctrl+V	**Video Menu** Displays a menu that lists various video clips of Cortez Peters showing championship techniques or providing background on his typing heritage.
Ctrl+X	**Exit** Exits the program. Not active within an exercise (press **Esc** to cancel the exercise first).
Esc	**Previous Menu** Cancels an exercise. If a scored exercise, the report is marked canceled.
F1	**Help** Opens Help.
F6	**Next** Moves to the next screen in an exercise.
Shft+F6	**Previous** Moves back to the previous screen in an exercise.

Chapter 4: Types of Exercises

Warmups

After the student logs on to the program, the first activity is a 5 minute Warmup. After exiting the Warmup, the student can go back to the Warmup exercise at any time by moving to the Main Menu and clicking the Previous button on the toolbar. For specific information on how the Warmup exercise works, see "The Warmup," pages 17-18.

5-Minute Timed Writings

5-Minute Timed Writings occur as a component of Pretests and Posttests and alone, as Supplemental 5-Minute Timed Writings. All timed writings work essentially the same way. They all are 5 minutes in duration, editing is not allowed, and word wrap is on. For any given timed writing, the student takes two attempts (unless the student achieves an honor roll paper, in which case CP3 allows the student to skip the second attempt). The student can restart either attempt one time only, and it must be within the first 30 seconds.

Here is how a timed writing works:

1. The student selects a timed writing in either of two ways:
   - Pretest/Posttest Button—select the Pretest/Posttest button on the Main Menu, select a particular Pretest or Posttest on the Pretest/Posttest Menu, and select 5-Minute Timed Writing in the selected Pretest/Posttest activity dialog box.
   - Supplemental 5-Minute Timed Writings Button—select Supplemental 5-Minute Timed Writings on the Main Menu and then select one of the timed writings on the Supplemental Timed Writings Menu.
2. The 5-Minute Timed Writing introduction/directions screen displays. The student turns to the appropriate page in the textbook (specified in the status bar at the bottom of the screen) and clicks the Next button on the toolbar to continue.
3. The 5-Minute Timed Writing input screen displays with the insertion point at the top of an empty scrolling window. When the student presses the first key, the 5-minute timer begins.

❖ **Note:** The time remaining (in whole minutes) displays in the status bar at the bottom of the screen.

4. The student types the text from the textbook. If finished keying the text before time is up, the student repeats the passage from the beginning. The student can cancel or restart the timed writing as follows:
   - During the first 30 seconds, the student can restart the current attempt by clicking the Restart button on the toolbar. The Restart button is active only one time per attempt and only during the first 30 seconds.
   - At any time during a timed writing, the student can cancel the timed writing entirely by clicking the Menu button on the toolbar. If the student cancels during the first attempt, the timed writing will be marked as "canceled" on the student's Report. To work on the timed writing subsequently, the student will start over. If the student cancels during the second attempt, the timed writing will be marked as complete and the student will not be able to return to the timed writing to work on the second attempt.
5. A dialog box announces when time is up. The student clicks **OK**.
6. The student's speed and error scores now appear in the dialog bar (above the input area). Another dialog box asks if the student wants to review scored text: the student clicks **No** to bypass the review or **Yes** (the default) to review scored text on screen.
7. On the review screen, the student's scored copy appears double-spaced in a scrolling window. To print the scored copy with score information, the student clicks the **Print** button. When finished reviewing the scored text, the student clicks the Next button on the toolbar.
8. After the student reviews the scored copy (or bypasses the review) for the first attempt, the second attempt is keyed, scored, and reviewed.

❖ **Note:** If the student earns an honor roll paper (see "Honor Rolls," below) on the first attempt at a timed writing, CP3 gives the student the option of skipping the second attempt.

9. When the timed writing is completed, CP3 charts the better of the two timings (see "Charting Timed Writings," page 45), showing the Speed and Accuracy Graph (Chart 1) first, followed by the Misstroke Analysis Chart (Chart 2). Pretest and Supple-

mental 5-Minute Timed Writings also include a list of recommended corrective practice exercises, which is accessible by clicking the **View Prescriptions** button on the Misstroke Analysis Chart screen. To print the graph or chart, the student clicks **Print**. To navigate among screens, the student uses the Next and Previous buttons on the toolbar.

❖ **Note:** The student can retake any completed Supplemental 5-Minute Timed Writing but cannot retake a completed Pretest/Posttest timed writing until all Pretests and Posttests have been completed.

Charting Timed Writings

The better of the two attempts will be used to create the Speed and Accuracy Graph (Chart 1) and the Misstroke Analysis (Chart 2). The better timing is determined as follows:

1. If both attempts have 5 errors or less, the one with the higher NWAM (net words a minute) is considered the better of the two. If the NWAMs are equal, the timing with the fewer errors is considered the better one.
2. If both attempts have more than 5 errors, the one with the fewer errors is considered the better one.
3. If the student made 5 errors or less in one attempt and more than 5 errors in a second attempt, the one with 5 errors or less is considered the better one.

For detailed information on the charting for timed writings, see "Speed and Accuracy Graph," pages 26-27, and "Misstroke Analysis Chart," pages 27-28.

Honor Rolls

The student can earn any one of three honor roll papers for a given timed writing, as follows:

- Accuracy Honor Roll: the student keys within 3 words a minute of the NWAM of the most recent timed writing, making 0 or 1 error.
- Speed Honor Roll: the student matches the NWAM of the most recent timed writing or exceeds it by up to 4 words a minute, making 0 or 1 error.
- Super Honor Roll: the student exceeds the NWAM of the most recent timed writing by at least 5 words a minute, making 0 or 1 error.

When the student earns an honor roll paper, a special honor roll animation plays and the student's score in the dialog bar (and on the Summary Report) appears with one star (Accuracy Honor Roll), two stars (Speed Honor Roll), or three stars (Super Honor Roll).

Diagnostic Tests

Diagnostic tests occur as a component of Pretests, a component of Posttests, and alone, as Supplemental Diagnostic Tests. All Diagnostic Tests function exactly the same. Each Diagnostic Test consists of a series of ten 1-minute timings. No editing is allowed and word wrap is off.

Here is how a Diagnostic Test works:

1. The student selects a Diagnostic Test in either of two ways:
   - Pretest/Posttest Button—select Pretest/Posttest on the Main Menu, select a particular Pretest or Posttest on the Pretest/ Posttest Menu, and select Diagnostic Test in the selected Pretest/Posttest activity dialog box.
   - Supplemental Diagnostic Tests Button—select Supplemental Diagnostic Tests on the Main Menu, then select one of the Diagnostic Tests from the Supplemental Diagnostic Tests Menu.
2. The introduction/directions screen displays. The student turns to the appropriate page in the textbook (specified in the status bar at the bottom of the screen) and clicks the Next button on the toolbar to continue.

❖ **Note:** Since the sentence is displayed on the screen, the student can key from the displayed line or from the textbook.

3. The first sentence appears at the top of the screen with an arrow pointing up under the first character in the sentence. The insertion point appears in the input area below the sentence. When the student keys the first character, the timer starts. The student keys the sentence, pressing **Enter** at the end of the sentence and repeating the sentence until time is up. As the student types, the arrow moves under the drill line sentence.
4. A dialog box announces when time is up. The student clicks OK and keys the next sentence in the Diagnostic Test.
5. The student completes the remaining sentences. At the end of the tenth sentence, a dialog box asks if the student wants to

review scored copy: the student clicks **Yes** (the default) to review scored copy or **No** to bypass the review screen.

6. On the review screen, the student's scored copy appears double-spaced in a scrolling window. Above each sentence is the student's GWAM (gross words a minute), errors, CWAM (correct words a minute), and the goal for the sentence. To print the scored copy with score information, the student clicks the **Print** button. When finished reviewing the scored text, the student clicks the Next button on the toolbar.

7. After the student completes the Diagnostic Test and review (if chosen), CP3 displays the Speed and Accuracy Analysis Chart (Chart 3). Pretest and Supplemental Diagnostic Tests include a list of recommended corrective practice exercises, which is accessible by clicking the **View Prescriptions** button on the chart screen. To print the chart, the student clicks **Print**.

❖ **Note:** If the student cancels a Diagnostic Test without completing all 10 sentences and then returns to the Diagnostic Test, CP3 takes the student to the sentence after the last completed sentence.

Skill-Development Paragraphs

The Skill-Development Paragraphs activity is intended to be done the last five to ten minutes of each corrective practice hour. In Skill-Development Paragraphs, word wrap is on and editing is disabled. The activity allows five or ten attempts per day, depending on the "Number of attempts on Skill-Development Paragraphs" setting in the selected options file. (For more information about options files, see "Setting Program Options," pages 10-13.)

❖ **Note:** Restarts count toward the per-day attempt total.

Here is how the Skill-Development Paragraphs activity works:

1. The student selects the Skill-Development Paragraphs button on the Main Menu.

2. The Skill-Development Paragraphs introduction/direction screen displays. The student turns to the appropriate textbook page (specified in the status bar at the bottom of the screen) and clicks the Next button on the toolbar.

3. The input screen displays with the insertion point at the top of an empty scrolling window. The dialog bar at the top of the

screen indicates the attempt number and paragraph level. When the student presses the first key, the 1-minute timer begins.

❖ **Note:** CP3 begins with the 20 WAM paragraph; subsequently, the paragraph level corresponds to the first Skill-Development Paragraph that the student has not typed in one minute error-free. You can override the paragraph level for a particular student, however, by accessing Instructor Options... on the Help pull-down menu. For more information, see "Correcting Log-on Information," pages 36-38.

4. The student keys the paragraph from the textbook.
   - At the first error, the program beeps and displays a large red X in the dialog bar. At this point, the student can continue keying the paragraph (to practice) or click the Restart button on the toolbar to begin keying the same paragraph over again. Each restart counts as an attempt.
   - If the student keys the full paragraph in one minute or less without any errors, a congratulations dialog box appears. The student clicks **OK** to begin the next paragraph level (unless the student has completed the maximum for that day)
   - If the student is still keying the paragraph when 1 minute has elapsed, a time-up dialog box displays. The student clicks **OK** to begin keying the same paragraph over again.

❖ **Note:** At any time, the student can cancel the activity by clicking the Menu button on the toolbar or pressing **Esc**. When this happens, the paragraph will be marked as incomplete on the Summary Report. The student can return later on the same day to resume the activity where he or she left off.

5. The student takes another 1-minute timing on either the current paragraph level (if the student did not complete it successfully in the previous attempt) or the next paragraph level. The activity continues for a total of either five or ten attempts (counting restarts). After the final attempt, a dialog box tells the student that he or she has completed the maximum number of attempts for the day. The student clicks **OK** to return to the Main Menu.

❖ **Note:** If you want a student to do more than the maximum number of attempts specified in the selected options file, have the student exit CP3 after reaching the maximum for the day and then log on again using an earlier date.

The student's progress in Skill-Development Paragraphs is recorded on Chart 4, which is accessible from the Charts pull-down menu.

For more information, see "Skill-Development Paragraph Record (Chart 4), page 33.

Rhythm Development Drills

There are two Rhythm Development drills, Sentences (composed of Simple Speed Sentences and Difficult Sentences) and Skillbuilding. The two drills constitute one side of a Cortez Peters Rhythm Development tape.

The Rhythm Development button appears on the Main Menu only if the "Include Rhythm Development Drills" is checked in the selected options file. The source of the audio for the Rhythm Development Sentences drills is also specified in the selected options file: if "Use WAV Files for Audio" is checked, the audio will be played from the CP3 CD-ROM; if it is not checked, the program assumes that you will play the audio from the Cortez Peters Rhythm Development Tapes (available from Glencoe separately).

❖ **Note:** If the student completes a Sentences drill, the corresponding tape/drill selection will be marked complete on the Rhythm Development Drill Menu. The student does not have to complete Skillbuilding to have completed the tape/drill. However, if the student completes Skillbuilding first, the corresponding tape/drill selection will be marked as partially complete. The student has to key the Sentences drill to have completed the tape/drill.

Rhythm Development Sentences

The Rhythm Development Sentences drill consist of a series of simple speed sentences followed by a series of difficult sentences. The student listens to Cortez Peters and types along with him stroke-for-stroke. The Rhythm Development Sentences drill is scored but not timed. Word wrap is off and editing is disabled.

Here is how the Rhythm Development Sentences drill works:

1. The student selects the Rhythm Development Drills button on the Main Menu.
2. The student chooses a drill from the Rhythm Development Drill Menu (the drill name corresponds to one side of a Cortez Peters Rhythm Development audiocassette) and clicks OK.
3. In the activity dialog box for the selected drill, the student clicks the Sentences button. Simple Speed Sentences will be keyed first, then Difficult Sentences.

4. The introduction/directions screen displays. The student clicks the Next button on the toolbar to continue.

❖ **Note:** The drill can be typed from the line displayed on screen or from the script in the Cortez Peters Rhythm Development Tapes package (ISBN 0-02-801204-6).

5. The first Simple Speed Sentence appears at the top of the screen, and the insertion point appears in a blank scrolling window below the sentence.
   - If you are using the Cortez Peters Rhythm Development Tapes (rather than the audio files on the CD-ROM version) for this drill, start the tape now.
   - If you are using the audio files on the CD-ROM, the Cortez Peters audio begins.
6. The student keys the sentence, matching Cortez Peters stroke-for-stroke. At the end of the sentence, the student's text is scored (for display later, at the end of the drill) and the program advances to the next sentence.

❖ **Note:** At the end of a drill line, Cortez Peters tells the student to either "Return, double space" or just "double space." For the former, the student should press **Enter** three times; for the latter, the student should press **Enter** two times.

7. The student continues typing the Sentences drill, matching the Cortez Peters audio. The drill is finished when both Simple Speed Sentences and Difficult Sentences have been keyed. At this point, the last Difficult Sentence is scored and the total number of errors for the completed Sentences drill is displayed in the dialog bar at the top of the screen. If the student earned a certificate (one star for 3 to 5 errors, two stars for 1 to 2 errors, and three stars for 0 errors), a special certificate animation plays.

❖ **Note:** At any time, the student can cancel the drill by clicking the Menu button on the toolbar or pressing **Esc**. When this happens, the drill will be marked as incomplete on the Summary Report and on the Rhythm Development Drill Menu. The student can return later to resume the drill where he or she left off (to the beginning of the first incomplete sentence) or to start it over from the beginning.

8. After the Sentences drill has been scored, a dialog box asks if the student wants to review scored text: the student clicks **OK** (the default) to review scored text on screen or **No** to bypass the review and return to the Rhythm Development Drill Menu.

9. On the review screen, the student's scored copy appears double-spaced in a scrolling window. The student can print the scored text by clicking the **Print** button. When finished reviewing scored text, the student clicks the Next button on the toolbar to return to the Rhythm Development Drill Menu.

Rhythm Development Skillbuilding

The Rhythm Development Skillbuilding drill is done only for practice before or after the student works on the Rhythm Development Sentences drill. The Rhythm Development Skillbuilding drill is unscored and untimed. Word wrap is off and editing is disabled.

Here is how the Rhythm Development Skillbuilding drill works:

1. The student selects the Rhythm Development Drills button on the Main Menu.
2. The student chooses a drill from the Rhythm Development Drill Menu (the drill name corresponds to one side of a Cortez Peters Rhythm Development audiocassette) and clicks **OK**.
3. In the activity dialog box for the selected drill, the student clicks the Skillbuilding button.
4. The introduction/directions screen displays. The student clicks the Next button on the toolbar to continue.
5. The first drill line appears at the top of the screen, and the insertion point appears in a blank scrolling window below the drill line. The student keys the drill line five times, pressing **Enter** at the end of each line.

❖ **Note:** The drill can be typed from the line displayed on screen or from the Cortez Peters Rhythm Development Tapes script.

6. The next drill line appears at the top of the screen. The student keys the second drill line five times, pressing **Enter** at the end of each line.
7. The student keys the remaining drill lines five times each. At the end of the drill, the program returns to the Rhythm Development Drill Menu.

Accuracy Studies

Accuracy Studies are assigned as corrective practice from Charts 2 and 3. They are designed to help the student make fewer errors at the keyboard. In each Accuracy Study drill, the student is required to key each drill line perfectly three times before advancing to the next drill line. Accuracy Study drills are untimed. Word wrap is off and editing is disabled.

Here is how an Accuracy Study drill works:

1. The student selects an Accuracy Study drill in either of two ways:
   - Corrective Practice Button—select the Corrective Practice button on the Main Menu, then select an Accuracy Study drill listed on the Corrective Practice Menu and click **OK**. The Accuracy Study drills listed on the Corrective Practice Menu are prescribed as a result of the student's most recent Pretest (5-Minute Timed Writing and/or Diagnostic Test).
   - Accuracy Studies Button—select the Accuracy Studies button on the Main Menu, then select a particular study and drill on the Accuracy Study Menu and click **OK**.

❖ Note: Accuracy Study drills are prescribed as a result of Pretest and Supplemental 5-Minute Timed Writings and Diagnostic Tests. Prescriptions for the most recent Pretest (5-Minute Timed Writing and/or Diagnostic Test) appear on the Corrective Practice Menu. Prescriptions for Supplemental 5-Minute Timed Writings are accessible from Chart 2, and prescriptions for Supplemental Diagnostic Tests are accessible from Chart 3. For more information, see "Misstroke-Analysis Chart (Chart 2)," pages 27-28, and "Speed and Accuracy Analysis Chart (Chart 3)," pages 30-33.

2. The introduction/directions screen displays. The student clicks the Next button on the toolbar to continue.

3. The first drill line appears at the top of the screen, and the insertion point appears in a blank scrolling window below the drill line.

❖ Note: Since the drill line is displayed on the screen, the student can key from the displayed line or from the textbook.

4. The student keys the drill line and presses **Enter**. The first time the student misstrokes, the program beeps and displays a large red X in the dialog bar. At this point, the student can continue keying the drill line (to practice) or press **Enter** to begin rekeying the same drill line. When the student keys the drill line without making any errors, the dialog bar adds 1 to the number correct for the current drill line and for the total number correct for the drill.

5. The student keys the drill line as many times as it takes to key it perfectly three times. After the third perfect keying of a drill line, a dialog box congratulates the student: the student clicks **OK** to begin working on the next drill line.

6. The student works through the remaining drill lines. For each line, the student must key the line perfectly three times before the program advances to the next line.

❖ **Note:** At any time, the student can cancel the drill by clicking the Menu button on the toolbar or pressing **Esc**. When this happens, the drill will be marked as incomplete on the Summary Report, the Accuracy Study Menu, and the Corrective Practice Menu (if the drill is listed there). The student can return later to resume the drill where he or she left off or to start it over from the beginning.

7. After the student keys the final drill perfectly three times, a dialog box asks if the student wants to review his or her copy: the student clicks **Yes** (the default) to review the copy or **No** to bypass the review screen and return to the previous menu.

8. On the review screen, the student's copy appears double-spaced in a scrolling window. To print the copy, the student clicks the **Print** button. When finished reviewing the copy, the student clicks the Next button on the toolbar to return to the previous menu.

When the student completes an Accuracy Study drill, that drill will be marked as complete on the Accuracy Study Menu. If the drill appears on the Corrective Practice Menu (that is, it was prescribed as a result of the most recent Pretest), it will also be marked as complete on the Corrective Practice Menu.

❖ **Note:** All completion marks for Accuracy Study drills are wiped out when a new Corrective Practice Menu is created, which happens when the student takes a 5-Minute Timed Writing or Diagnostic Test for a new Pretest. Clearing completion marks allows the student to keep track of his or her work based on only the most recently prescribed corrective practice.

Speed Studies

Speed Studies are assigned as corrective practice from Chart 3. They are designed to help the student improve keyboarding speed. In each Speed Study drill, the student is required to key each drill line perfectly five times before advancing to the next drill line. Speed Study drills are untimed. Word wrap is off and editing is disabled.

Here is how a Speed Study drill works:

1. The student selects a Speed Study drill in either of two ways:
   - Corrective Practice Button—select the Corrective Practice button on the Main Menu, then select a Speed Study drill listed on the Corrective Practice Menu and click **OK**. The Speed Study drills listed on the Corrective Practice Menu are prescribed as a result of the student's most recent Pretest Diagnostic Test.
   - Speed Studies Button—select the Speed Studies button the Main Menu, then select a particular study and drill on the Speed Study Menu and click **OK**.

❖ **Note:** Speed Study drills are prescribed as a result of Pretest and Supplemental Diagnostic Tests. Prescriptions for the most recent Pretest Diagnostic Test appear on the Corrective Practice Menu. Prescriptions for Supplemental Diagnostic Tests are accessible from Chart 3. For more information, see "Speed and Accuracy Analysis Chart (Chart 3)," pages 30-33.

2. The introduction/directions screen displays. The student clicks the Next button on the toolbar to continue.

3. The first drill line appears at the top of the screen, and the insertion point appears in a blank scrolling window below the drill line.

❖ **Note:** Since the drill line is displayed on the screen, the student can key from the displayed line or from the textbook.

4. The student keys the drill line and presses **Enter**. The first time the student misstrokes, the program beeps and displays a large red X in the dialog bar. At this point, the student can continue keying the drill line (to practice) or press **Enter** to begin rekeying the same drill line. When the student keys the drill line without making any errors, the dialog bar adds 1 to the number correct for the current drill line and for the total number correct for the drill.

5. The student keys the drill line as many times as it takes to key it perfectly five times. After the fifth perfect keying of a drill line, a dialog box congratulates the student: the student clicks **OK** to begin working on the next drill line.

6. The student works through the remaining drill lines. For each line, the student must key the line perfectly five times before the program advances to the next line.

❖ **Note:** At any time, the student can cancel the drill by clicking the Menu button on the toolbar or pressing **Esc**. When this happens, the drill will be marked as incomplete on the Summary Report, the Speed Study Menu, and the Corrective Practice Menu (if the drill is listed there). The student can return later to resume the drill where he or she left off or to start it over from the beginning.

7. After the student keys the final drill perfectly five times, a dialog box asks if the student wants to review his or her copy: the student clicks **Yes** (the default) to review the copy or **No** to bypass the review screen and return to the previous menu.

8. On the review screen, the student's copy appears double-spaced in a scrolling window. To print the copy, the student clicks the **Print** button. When finished reviewing the copy, the student clicks the Next button on the toolbar to return to the previous menu.

When the student completes a Speed Study drill, that drill will be marked as complete on the Speed Study Menu. If the drill appears on the Corrective Practice Menu (that is, it was prescribed as a result of the most recent Pretest Diagnostic Test), it will also be marked as complete on the Corrective Practice Menu.

❖ **Note:** All completion marks for Speed Study drills are wiped out when a new Corrective Practice Menu is created, which happens when the student takes a Diagnostic Test for a new Pretest. Clearing completion marks allows the student to keep track of his or her work based on only the most recently prescribed corrective practice.

Misspelled Words

The Misspelled Words drill provides a way for students to practice problematic words. The drill is untimed and unscored. Word wrap is off and editing is disabled.

Here is how the Misspelled Words drill works:

1. The student clicks the Corrective Practice button on the Main Menu.

2. On the Corrective Practice Menu, the student selects Misspelled Words and clicks OK.

❖ **Note:** Misspelled Words is accessible only from the Corrective Practice Menu, which always lists the Misspelled Words drill (even if the student has not taken a Pretest), but not the misspelled words themselves. Selecting Misspelled Words enables the student to access a blank practice screen.

3. The introduction/directions screen displays. The student clicks the Next button on the toolbar to continue.

4. The input screen includes a blank, scrolling window. The student keys the problematic words from 5-Minute Timed Writings, Diagnostic Tests, and Skill-Development Paragraphs. (Cortez Peters recommends keying each misspelled word correctly 25 times.)

❖ **Note:** CP3 does not identify problem words for the student. Rather, the student should print a copy of the Detailed Report for the Timed Writing, Diagnostic Test, or Skill-Development Paragraph and identify misspelled words from the Detailed Report. For more information, see "Viewing and Printing Reports," pages 33-35.

5. When finished practicing problem words, the student clicks the Next button on the toolbar to return to the Corrective Practice Menu. To go back to the Main Menu from there, the student clicks the Menu button on the toolbar.

Appendix: Troubleshooting Guide

If you have any questions or problems as you install program files or work with student work files, first make sure that your system meets the requirements outlined in "System Requirements," page 3, and that you followed the exact procedure outlined in "Installation," pages 5-9. Next, check this troubleshooting guide. If you experience a problem not covered here or not remedied by following a suggestion listed here, record exactly where you were and what happened when you or the student encountered the problem. Then call Glencoe's customer software support center at **1-800-437-3715** (8:30-4:00 ET).

❖ **Note:** If you suspect that you have a defective disk, do not modify it in any way. Glencoe will not be responsible for disks that have been recopied, reformatted, or purchased from a source other than Glencoe.

■ **When installing CP3, the Select Installation Drive... dialog box indicates that the drive does not have sufficient free space.**

Explanation. CP3 requires 7MB of free hard-disk space, which the selected drive does not have.

Suggestion: If you have another hard disk drive with at least 7MB of free space, select that other drive and click **OK** to continue the CP3 installation. Otherwise, press **Esc** to cancel the installation, then free space on your hard disk and run the CP3 installation again.

■ **When starting the program, a dialog box displays an Error E001 message.**

Explanation 1: CP3 is looking for a data disk in the floppy drive A: or floppy drive B: (as indicated in the name of the CP3 program icon) but there is no CP3 data disk in the floppy drive.

Suggestion: Insert a CP3 data disk (available from Glencoe) in the floppy drive before you start the program. If you want to store student data in a different location, you need to run the set-up program to create a data directory and program icon for each student. See "Setting Up Student Data Files," pages 9-10.

Explanation 2: The data disk is defective.

Suggestion: Call Glencoe customer support.

- **When starting the program, a dialog box displays an Error E002 message.**

  Explanation 1: CP3 cannot find the data directory specified in the Command Line for the program icon used to start CP3.

  Suggestion: If you run the set-up program to create a program icon and data directory, the correct Command Line will be used. See "Setting Up Student Data Files," pages 9-10.

- **When starting the CD-ROM version of CP3 and advancing from the title and copyright screens, an Application Error message appears or a video window appears but a video clip does not play.**

  Explanation: Microsoft Video for Windows has not been installed on the computer, or an incompatible version of Microsoft Video for Windows is installed.

  Suggestion: Use the VfW Setup icon in the Cortez Peters Keyboarding program group to install Microsoft Video for Windows. Then restart your computer before using CP3. For more information, see page 7.

- **The Log-on Information screen has the same name for each student.**

  Explanation: Students are not using their own data disks. A used data disk may have been copied for other students.

  Suggestion: Make sure each student starts with a new, unique set of student data disks.

- **A student forgot his or her password and cannot get into the program.**

  Explanation: You cannot view the student's original password, but you can create a new one for the student. See "Correcting Log-on Information," pages 36-37.

- **A message indicates that the data disk is full.**

  Explanation: The student is about to exceed the available disk space on the data disk and needs to free disk space before continuing.

  Suggestion: When this message appears, click **OK** to close the message dialog box. Exit CP3 and make a copy of the full data disk, if you wish. Then restart CP3, log on, and select *Delete Files...* on the File pull-down menu. In the Delete Detailed Report Files dialog box, choose one or more files to delete and click on **OK**. In the Confirm dialog box, click **Yes** or **Yes to All** to delete the selected files. When you delete Detailed Report files, you delete text only. Scores for exercises with deleted text are retained on the Summary Report.

- **A message indicates that the Summary Report file is full.**

  Explanation: The maximum number of exercises that can be listed on a Summary Report is 500. When the Summary Report exceeds 500 exercises, the program automatically overwrites exercises starting with the oldest first. When this happens, you will not be able to access old exercises that are overwritten on the Summary Report.

  Suggestion: Make a copy of the data disk (or data directory), to have in case you want to access old exercises that will not be accessible when CP3 is used in the future. Then continue using CP3.

- **Scored copy contains numerous "<¶>" or "{¶}" marks.**

  Explanation: the student did not follow the word wrap setting indicated in the exercise header at the top of the screen. A "<¶>" occurs in scored copy where word wrap is off and the student fails to press **Enter** at the end of the line. A "{¶}" occurs in scored copy where word wrap is on and the student mistakenly presses **Enter** at the end of the line.

  Suggestion: Retype the exercise following the word wrap setting in the exercise header.

Index

I

K

L

M

N

O

P

R

S

T

U

V

W